All I Have Is Them

Life with lives

Cannio Cardozo

authorHOUSE

AuthorHouse™
1663 Liberty Drive
Bloomington, IN 47403
www.authorhouse.com
Phone: 833-262-8899

© 2025 Cannio Cardozo. All rights reserved.

No part of this book may be reproduced, stored in a retrieval system, or transmitted by any means without the written permission of the author.

Published by AuthorHouse 08/20/2025

ISBN: 979-8-8230-4881-1 (sc)
ISBN: 979-8-8230-4880-4 (e)

Library of Congress Control Number: 2025908538

Print information available on the last page.

Any people depicted in stock imagery provided by Getty Images are models, and such images are being used for illustrative purposes only.
Certain stock imagery © Getty Images.

This book is printed on acid-free paper.

Because of the dynamic nature of the Internet, any web addresses or links contained in this book may have changed since publication and may no longer be valid. The views expressed in this work are solely those of the author and do not necessarily reflect the views of the publisher, and the publisher hereby disclaims any responsibility for them.

Acknowledgment

First and foremost, I express my heartfelt gratitude to Almighty God for His abundant blessings and inspiration that have guided me throughout my writing journey.

I sincerely thank Rev. Fr. Silvestre D'Souza, Provincial Superior of the Karnataka-Goa Province, for granting the necessary permissions and for graciously presenting my book with a foreword. I am also deeply grateful to Rev. Fr. Alexander Braganza, Provincial Delegate to Canada, for his constant support.

My appreciation extends to my community members, Fr. Steny Mascarenhas and Fr. Jeevan Dalmeida, for their unwavering encouragement. I also express my heartfelt thanks to Fr. Lawrence D'Mello, Fr. Iven D'Souza, and Fr. Rathan Nicholas Almeida for generously offering their time and valuable suggestions.

Last but not least, I would like to thank AuthorHouse Book Publishers for their invaluable assistance in making this book a reality.

Foreword

At the beginning of last year, I had the joy of writing a foreword to the author's second book: *All I have is you*. Within a short time he has completed the trilogy, with a new thought-provoking volume, and an apt title: *"All I have is Them."* He surely does not have a magic wand, to keep doling out such resources. They require study, reflection and introspection. Many of us who know his cheerful and bubbly nature - especially as a seminarian - marvel as to how he has managed to sit at the desk and discipline himself to put such sublime thoughts into print for a larger audience.

The reader is captured by his direct and convincing approach. The book manifests how well-versed he is with the topics dealt. By "them" reference is made to all the fauna and flora by which humans are surrounded; in which they live and move and breathe and swim and fly. Examples are taken from ancient civilizations to show how health and happiness follow good human rrelations with nature and the world of nature. Throughout the book, the importance of ecology is emphasized. Human beings must RESPECT God's creation and be RESPONSIBLE for it.

Pope Francis of happy memory, was the first to publish a Papal Encyclical dedicated fully to nature, environment and ecology: *Laudato Si* (24th May, 2015), in which he lovingly refers to the earth as *"our common home."* He followed it up with an Apostolic Exhortation: *Laudate Deum* on the climate crisis (4th October, 2023). We are grateful to him for addressing such a pressing issue, which affects our lives.

Our Carmelite Saints, including Sts Teresa of Avila and John of the Cross, have been lovers of nature. It is reflected in their writings and poems. Fr Cannio is following in their footsteps. I congratulate him for taking a cue from Pope Francis and our Holy Parents and emphasizing the values towards nature, that demand our urgent attention today. May your talent for creative and useful literature bloom further! May God bless your sincere efforts to promote the values enshrined in the Gospel and make of you a modern evangelizer!

Fr Silvestre D'Souza OCD
Provincial Superior
Karnataka-Goa Province
Order of Discalced Carmelites

General Introduction

In my debut work, *All I Have Is I*, I explored our bond with material things. My second book, *All I Have Is You*, examines how individuals connect with other human beings. In *All I Have Is Them*, the book shifts its focus to how we relate with flora and fauna, and underlines our responsibility toward them.

The Bible beautifully emphasizes that human beings are the crown of God's creation and entrusted with a unique role and responsibility within the world. Pope John Paul II, in his 1990 World Day of Peace message, *Peace with God the Creator, Peace with All of Creation*, reinforces this idea by reflecting on the book of Genesis, where God's creation is repeatedly described as "good." Yet the creation of humanity led to a revised evaluation of "very good" (Gen. 1:31), showcasing the unique value of human beings.

He states, "Adam and Eve's call to share in the unfolding of God's plan of creation brought into play those abilities and gifts which distinguish the human being from all other creatures. At the same time, their call established a fixed relationship between humankind and the rest of creation. Made in the image and likeness of God, Adam and Eve were to have exercised their dominion over the earth with wisdom and love" (Gen. 1:28). This emphasizes humanity's unique position, not just as part of creation but as its entrusted caretaker.

God's rest on the seventh day (Gen. 2:3) signifies the completion and perfection of creation, with human beings as its stewards. However, this divine entrustment does not grant humans unlimited control over nature; rather, their dominion must be exercised with wisdom, responsibility, and deep respect for God's creation. John Paul II's message advocated for a more ethical treatment of the earth, highlighting the link between peace with God and peace with the world. Humanity's acceptance of this role ensures environmental harmony, fulfilling its divine duty as creation's stewards.

Human beings, while recognized as the crown of creation, do not have a license to exploit other living creatures. Instead, their calling is to be caretakers of creation, responsible for its protection and upkeep. Pope Benedict XVI, in his 2010 World Day of Peace message *If You Want to Cultivate Peace, Protect Creation*, affirms this by emphasizing that nature is not a product of blind chance but originates from God's plan of love and truth. The book of Genesis shows that creation, born of God's wisdom, finds its purpose in humankind, created in God's likeness. However, the harmony between God, humanity, and creation was disrupted by sin as Adam and Eve sought to take the place of God, leading to selfishness, exploitation, and disorder in the natural world. The true meaning of God's command to "have dominion" over the earth (Gen. 1:28) was never about absolute control but a call to responsibility. He says, "The *Book of Genesis*, in its very first pages, points to the wise design of the cosmos: it comes forth from God's mind and finds its culmination in man and woman, made in the image and likeness of the Creator to 'fill the earth and to have dominion over it as stewards of God himself'" (cf. Gen 1:28). Nature is not to be treated as a mere resource for reckless use but as a gift from the Creator, entrusted to humanity with an inherent order and purpose. As such, human beings must act as coworkers with God, not as tyrants over creation, ensuring that they cultivate and care for the earth with wisdom and reverence.

Pope Francis, in his famous encyclical *Laudato Si'*, beautifully refers to creation as our "common home," emphasizing our shared responsibility to care for it. He states, "The urgent challenge to protect our common home includes a concern to bring the whole human family together to seek a sustainable and integral development, for we know that things can change." If creation is the common home, then every creature is related to each other. This he stresses in *Laudato Si'*, by quoting the hymn of Saint Francis of Assisi.

> Praised be you, my Lord, with all your creatures,
> especially Sir Brother Sun,
> who is the day and through whom you give us light.
> And he is beautiful and radiant with great splendour;
> and bears a likeness of you, Most High.
> Praised be you, my Lord, through Sister Moon and the stars,
> in heaven you formed them clear and precious and beautiful.
> Praised be you, my Lord, through Brother Wind,
> and through the air, cloudy and serene, and every kind of weather
> through whom you give sustenance to your creatures.
> Praised be you, my Lord, through Sister Water,
> who is very useful and humble and precious and chaste.
> Praised be you, my Lord, through Brother Fire,
> through whom you light the night,
> and he is beautiful and playful and robust and strong.

By quoting this hymn, Pope Francis highlights the sacred bond between humanity and the natural world, calling for a deep sense of reverence toward flora, fauna, and the environment. This perspective reinforces the call in *Laudato Si'* for ecological awareness and responsibility. Pope Francis urges humanity to embrace an attitude of gratitude and stewardship, recognizing that all of creation is interconnected. His message invites and challenges us, emphasizing that true faith requires both prayer and the protection of our shared environment.

Pope Francis highlights the urgent challenge of safeguarding our common home, stressing the need for global solidarity and sustainable development. He reassures us that the Creator does not abandon His creation, nor does He forsake His loving plan. Despite the environmental crises we face, humanity still has the power to work together in restoring balance and healing the earth. The Pope expresses deep gratitude to those dedicated to addressing environmental degradation, particularly those who fight to protect the most vulnerable communities who suffer its worst consequences.

He also recognizes young people's impassioned calls for change, questioning how a better future is possible without environmental action and social justice. Their call for justice serves as a powerful reminder that caring for creation is not just an ecological duty but a moral imperative for present and future generations.

As rational beings, it is our moral responsibility to acknowledge and respond to the needs of other creatures, both flora and fauna. In contrast to other life forms, humans have the intelligence and morality to acknowledge their environmental impact. Yet this capacity hasn't prevented our repeated failure to prioritize the environment, instead we favor self-interest.

This book's structure takes us on a journey of awareness and accountability. Part one explores the fundamental value of all living beings and their essential role in preserving our ecosystem's balance. This section will foster a deeper appreciation for how life is interconnected, stressing that nature deserves respect and care as our shared home, not just a resource to exploit.

The second part will address the devastating impact of human actions—greed, recklessness, and unsustainable practices—on countless species and ecosystems. We can find ways to heal our relationship with nature by acknowledging the harm we've caused to animals. This book encourages sustainable and compassionate living by prompting reflection and inspiring responsible action.

As in my previous two books, this one will also conclude each chapter with a poem. These poems will serve as a summary, helping to encapsulate the essence of each chapter in a meaningful and reflective way.

PART I

Introduction

If not for them, we would not have survived. From the smallest to the most prominent, every creature has a role to play in sustaining life—whether it's a tiny bee or an enormous baobab tree. The bee is instrumental in pollination, while the baobab is a true "tree of life," supporting countless species. The connection between humans and other living beings is deeper and more intricate than we often realize—an invisible yet undeniable bond.

For instance, the very breath we take depends entirely on plants. Though unseen, this exchange of oxygen and carbon dioxide is essential for our existence. This part delves into the profound and positive relationship between humans and the natural world—both flora and fauna.

Early humans lived in harmony with nature, abiding by its laws and treating plants and animals as members of their extended family. Even when hunting or gathering, they did so with reverence, understanding the delicate balance of life.

The interdependence of flora and fauna is almost supernatural, like a vast network of nerves sustaining life itself. Each being plays a crucial part, ensuring the survival of others in a delicate, interconnected web.

This section will illuminate the importance and immense value of flora and fauna through various examples. In one way or another, it will help us recognize their significance in our lives and deepen our appreciation for the crucial role they play in sustaining life. By exploring these relationships, we can better understand how interconnected we are with nature and why preserving it is essential for our well-being and survival.

Let me quote Gautama Buddha: "Besides respecting human life, we must also extend our compassion to animals and plants. That is true humanitarianism." He did not say this lightly, for he was a wise man who understood the true value of flora and fauna. His words reflect a deep understanding of the interconnectedness of all living beings and the responsibility humans have toward nature. True humanitarianism goes beyond just caring for fellow humans; it encompasses the protection and respect of all forms of life. Animals and plants are essential to the balance of the world, contributing to the well-being of the planet and, ultimately, to human survival. By acknowledging their worth, we embrace a more compassionate and sustainable way of living. Buddha's wisdom serves as a timeless reminder that kindness, respect, and care should not be confined to humanity alone but should extend to every living being that shares this world with us.

Chapter 1

The Womb

Let me begin this chapter with a quote from St. John Paul II.

> The aesthetic value of creation cannot be overlooked. Our very contact with nature has a deep restorative power; contemplation of its magnificence imparts peace and serenity. The Bible speaks again and again of the goodness and beauty of creation, which is called to glorify God.

The intricate balance and interconnectedness of God's creation reveal a masterful plan. All living and nonliving things together create a harmonious whole, like a nurturing womb.

At conception, sparks ignite the womb with life, transforming it into the cradle of human existence. The womb provides sustenance, protection, and development for the embryo.

This womb like concept is beautifully reflected in nature. Often referred to as "Mother Nature," it sustains all living things. The womb of this "Mother" is comprised of flora and fauna, with humankind as the embryo. Everything in creation—except humankind—exists seamlessly within this nurturing framework. This interconnected system is why I call nature a womb.

The power of thought, unique to humankind, places us on a higher pedestal, yet we remain entirely dependent on nature for our survival. The plant and animal kingdoms nurture and nourish us, allowing us to live;

they're essential to our survival, much like a womb protects a developing embryo. Our intelligence doesn't negate our connection to creation's origin; this delicate, life-sustaining system deserves our respect and safeguarding.

They are the reason for our survival, yet we ignore them. We are all connected as one. Here I would like to quote Albert Einstein.

> A human being is a part of the whole called by us universe, a part limited in time and space. He experiences himself, his thoughts and feeling as something separated from the rest, a kind of optical illusion of his consciousness. This delusion is a kind of prison for us, restricting us to our personal desires and to affection for a few persons nearest to us. Our task must be to free ourselves from this prison by widening our circle of compassion to embrace all living creature and the whole of nature in its beauty.

He makes a decisive point about human perception. Time and again, we distinguish ourselves as separate entities distinct from the rest of living things. This false perception, for Einstein, is an "optical delusion." Our consciousness interprets reality, but it does not mean it is the ultimate truth. Actually our rational faculty should have assisted us to be more considerate toward flora and fauna than to think we are special for our reason and disrespect or exploit other living things.

In the following section, we will explore the invaluable benefits that flora and fauna provide to humanity. In countless ways, nature's complex web of life supports us, from the air we breathe to the food we consume. Similarly, animals are essential to balance ecosystems, contributing to pollination, soil health, and even our emotional well-being.

Beyond basic needs, nature profoundly enhances our well-being physically, emotionally, and spiritually. Lush forests, flowing waters, and birdsongs bring peace and renewal.

Yet despite these profound gifts, we often take flora and fauna for granted, failing to recognize their roles in our existence. Let's consider nature's countless ways of sustaining us as we proceed.

Longing of Lungs

Every second our nostrils feel it, inhale it, with no pay. It is pumped in without consciousness most of the time, yet it is invaluable. It is not visible but enables our hearts to beat. If it bids goodbye to us, a creepy cold will take over our bodies and let us decay.

By now you've likely figured out it's oxygen. As we all know, flora plays an essential role in the oxygen cycle. Through the process of photosynthesis, the plants absorb carbon dioxide from the air, energy from the sunlight, and water from the ground. This results in food production for the plant and oxygen. If there were no plants, then we would cease to exist. The trade of gases among living beings sustains life on earth and forms the foundation for the interdependence between humans and trees.

Martin Luther King Jr. wisely said, "For in the true nature of things, if we rightly consider, every green tree is far more glorious than if it were made of gold and silver." The trees also enhance the quality of the air by filtering contaminants. The trees break down detrimental substances to provide pure air to breathe. This sanitation is important as it preserves the human respiratory system from atmospheric toxins.

Flora stores the excess carbon dioxide from the atmosphere as biomass and acts as one of the carbon sinks. This leads to the reduction of greenhouse gases in the air, which in turn benefits the locomotive living beings, which can enjoy the stable climate and wholesome environment for breathing.

Forest breathing is a term usually used regarding the psychological impact a stroll in the woods causes on human beings. The aftermath of this is visible in a revived mood and reduction in stress, and it provides improved mental health. This practice of planting your feet on the frosty land improves the respiratory system by formulating a healthier breathing pattern. Every breath we take is an insignificant act but a precious gift that we must esteem and cherish.

On the outskirts of a city was a hill, and it had a considerable cliff. One side was painted with shades of green and offered a breathtaking view of the village nestled in the soothing terrain below. On the other side, the cliff looked at the concert jungle of the city.

One bright day before the sun had blended into the mountains, a man walked toward the cliff from the side of the village and another man walked from the boisterous city. The former arrived on the cliff to take deep breaths. He sat down and contemplated life. The one who had come from the city came to take his breath away. The villager came in search of pure air and to enjoy every moment of life by deeply inhaling and exhaling the fresh air. The city dweller owned all the best facilities he could under the sun. He couldn't cope with the situation, because competition occupied his mind. He thought the only solution was to jump from the cliff and commit suicide.

People sometimes prioritize worldly things over their own breath. People often take breathing for granted. Every breath we take gets oxygen into our lungs, which enables us to live and move, and this is what I call the longing of lungs. Without oxygen, life as we know it would cease to exist.

Famished Stomach

I got this title from an incident that took place in my school. It was probably when Sam was in his primary school. He had participated in the fancy dress competition. He covered himself with torn clothes to project himself as a beggar. The range of participants was worth watching. One appeared as god, and another was a witch. If one was standing as a strong tree, the other would be a fallen log with no leaves as the repercussion of the deformation. If one dressed as the lion, a sign of pride, another had a costume of an elephant with broken tusks that were stolen for the ivory.

It was a coincidence that Sam and another had dressed as beggars. As the participants performed on the stage, they stood back in a line. Including the second beggar, there were five participants on the stage. During Sam's performance, he turned to the other beggar and humorously quipped, "First of all, I am hungry and begging, so don't expect anything from me." His witty remark drew chuckles from the audience, setting the stage for what was to come.

Captivated by Sam's performance, the judges asked the first beggar, "What's your plan if given money?" Without hesitation, the first beggar replied, "I would buy food for myself." It was a straightforward answer, reflecting the immediate necessity of sustenance.

Then it became Sam's turn to answer. A judge questioned him, "In the event of receiving food, what is your proposed course of action?" With wisdom beyond his years and a heart full of empathy, Sam replied, "I know the pain of a famished stomach, so I will share the food with the other beggar."

His sincere answer created a powerful emotional connection with the audience and judges. It spoke volumes about compassion and selflessness—qualities that transcended the boundaries of mere performance. Sam, playing the beggar, won over the audience at that very moment.

Yes, the famished stomach is a dominant sign of our primary requirement for nourishment. Hunger is a feeling experienced by everyone. It's often at the moment of extreme hunger that we genuinely recognize the crucial source of our living. The ultimate source of our food lies in the flora and fauna. The plants and animals supply us with the nutritional essentials for our survival.

Throughout history, humans have depended on the generosity of nature for our livelihood. Our ancestors walked miles in search of food. As nomads, they halted at a particular place till the food of that place was gone. They hit the road in an unknown direction just to feed their stomachs. They are the ones who knew the importance of flora and fauna.

However, when they learned the art of cultivation, they began to settle in a particular area. Consequently, civilization gradually evolved, and hunting weapons advanced. Their farming methods also developed. This led to the tendency of taking the source of nourishment for granted.

In the twenty-first century, when convenience often takes priority, it's become easy to ignore the utmost significance of the source of our food. We may grab a quick bite or order the food without paying attention to its origin. When we are famished, we only think about where to get the food.

Street children, the homeless, and beggars will demonstrate the urgent need for food. Our hunger is a constant reminder of our dependence on flora and fauna. It urges us to reflect on our interconnectedness with other living creatures in the ecosystems.

The famished stomach is not just a physical realization but a symbol of our dependence on the womb, which we have talked about earlier. We are called to cultivate an appreciation for the food we consume. This awareness should inspire us to make mindful choices that encourage the practice of reducing food waste and preserve the resources that provide us with livelihood.

The Body's Cocoon

In fact, clothes serve as a shielding cocoon for our body. Similarly, as a caterpillar encloses itself in a silken case for the period of metamorphosis, we too swathe ourselves in a textile that protects and keeps us safe.

One of my companions lived in a small village nestled between rolling hills and vegetables farms. The natural world spellbound his sister, Rena, around her from the exciting butterflies in her backyard.

One sunny day, Rena decided to explore the nearby woods. As she wandered into the thick forest, she spotted a caterpillar creeping its way along a branch. Being a future student of entomology, she cautiously picked up the caterpillar and placed it in a pot to monitor its transformation.

As days passed by, she marveled as the caterpillar spun a silky cocoon around itself. She wondered at how the caterpillar had transformed its body into a protective exterior, just like humans clothe themselves for protection.

Weeks passed by, and Rena diligently attended to the cocoon every day, ensuring its protection and uninterrupted growth. At last, one spring morning, she noticed a petite hole in the cocoon. The butterfly was prepared to appear! Rena held her breath as she witnessed the fragile creature grapple to break free from its silky coat.

With a tender flap, the butterfly came out, its wings unfurling to divulge vibrant shades of red and black. Rena was in seventh heaven as she witnessed the miraculous conversion from a caterpillar to a stunning butterfly.

As she freed the butterfly into the air, Rena understood the insightful lesson hidden in this natural spectacle. As she observed, Rena couldn't help but draw parallels between the caterpillar's cocoon and the clothes she wore every day. We are born naked as the caterpillar she saw first. Similar to how the caterpillar adorns itself with a cocoon, we also dress ourselves once we are born. The transformation is death. We leave our clothes and old body and transform into a distinct form, leaving to life after death.

She also realized, just like the caterpillar's cocoon provided protection during its metamorphosis, clothes were more than just fabric; clothes were not just a style projection but self-expression. They shielded her from the burning sun and from the cool winds.

In that moment, Rena understood the true essence of her clothing. It was not just about fashion or trend; it was about resilience and adaptableness. From that day on, Rena wore her clothes with a deep appreciation, and she also valued the source of the fabric.

Clothing holds immense significance in numerous aspects of human life. It shields from all whims of external elements. While human intelligence is responsible for manufacturing and designing clothes, the raw materials are sourced from plant fibers and animal skins, respectively.

Clothing acts as the principal layer of cover against environmental conditions, such as extreme fluctuations in temperature. It assists the body in regulating temperature, igniting warmth in the wintry day, and in the dog days of summer, it prevents the skin from sunburn. Fitting clothes enhances our overall comfort by reducing physical discomfort.

Clothing plays a key role in expressing a person's identity and cultural legacy. The individual's dressing style often reflects their beliefs, principles, and socioeconomic status. Various ethnicities have diverse traditional clothing styles that denote cultural pride, ceremonies, and rituals, fostering a sense of belongingness to a community. In professional functions, apt attire is essential for creating an optimistic impression and showing professionalism. Uniforms and dress codes convey respect for the context and reveal loyalty to social norms and expectations. Besides their usefulness, clothing also serves as a safeguard against the probable awkwardness of nakedness, a social norm embedded throughout the centuries.

Clothing also creates a great level of psychological impact. It boosts the individual with self-confidence and self-esteem. It is very well said that the first impression is the best impression. Dressing well allows a person to display a positive self-image. Even the attire the person is wearing plays a great role in the society indirectly through the light of the status of the person. Therefore, the well-dressed person most of the time will feel comfortable and dominant among others.

Clothing supports the individual in a specific function or occasion, such as sportswear for physical activities, protective gear for unsafe environments, and appropriate clothing for the mentally challenged and differently abled. These customized clothes enhance performance, safety, and comfort for various individuals.

Nature was crucial for ancient humans' survival, providing materials for clothing and adornment. Early clothing and accessories were made directly from plants and animals, highlighting nature's importance in early fashion.

Among the earliest clothing were animal hides and furs, offering warmth and protection from the elements. Through tanning, animal skins were turned into tough materials suitable for garments, shoes, and housing. Decorative essentials and sewing/weaving tools were often made from bones, teeth, and feathers.

Plants also played a vital role. Flax, cotton, and hemp were cultivated, woven into cloth, and dyed with natural pigments from leaves, roots, and flowers. They used bark, reeds, and grasses to create hats, footwear, and other accessories.

Early humans' ingenuity and resourcefulness were highlighted by their deep connection with nature. Their inventiveness with readily available materials provided for their basic needs and launched the evolution of fashion and skilled crafts. Clothing made from plants and animals reveals our connection to nature, a bond that still impacts our lives.

Stake to Flesh and Bones

Medicine acts as the stake to flesh and bones. A stake is often linked with something that is used to secure or support a composition. In terms of grading, it is a strong wooden or metal post with a point at one end, driven into the ground to support a tree or plant. Here, the stake serves as a metaphorical support for the flesh and bones. Medicine acts as the stake to a sick, vulnerable human being to fight and regain strength.

In the area of healthcare, the function of medicine is parallel to a robust stake supporting a structure, securing the health of a patient against the allure of foreign entities. This metaphor gains meaning when considering the broader perspective of human well-being and the threat projected by diseases and viruses. Conventional medicine classifications like Traditional Chinese Medicine and Ayurveda in Indian context greatly depend on plant and animal products for cures.

Ancient first aid heavily featured plant remedies, showcasing ancestral knowledge and a profound nature connection. Thinking back on my childhood, one vivid memory stands out—a moment that showcased the miraculous healing power of the natural world.

Summers were simpler then, spent entirely outdoors. My friends and I had countless adventures: playing cricket, berry picking, swimming, and appreciating the pristine natural beauty surrounding us. The paddy field was our favorite playground. We fashioned a makeshift cricket pitch from the uneven laterite soil and stones during the off-season.

Lost in a lively cricket match one afternoon, I ran to catch the ball. I lost my footing on the irregular terrain, resulting in a hard fall onto the rough ground. Deep gashes formed on my elbow and knee from scraping against sharp stones. Blood poured from my wounds, forming a pool around me as I sat there, shocked and in pain.

One of the older players, calm and quick-witted, sprang into action. He told them not to move and then rushed to the field's edge. Moments later, he reappeared, carrying milky sap harvested from a nearby Macaranga peltata tree, valued for its medicine. Gently, he applied the sap to my wounds. At first, it stung slightly but then, almost magically, the bleeding began to stop. My pain subsided, bringing a wave of relief.

With quiet reverence, he explained the tree's unique qualities. People have used its milk to heal wounds for generations. It's like nature's own bandage.

The fall left its mark, but more significantly, that day instilled in me a deep appreciation for the natural remedies available to us. The Macaranga peltata tree, standing tall at the edge of the field, became more than just a part of the landscape; it became a symbol of resilience, healing, and the wisdom of the past.

With hindsight, the extent of our reliance on the knowledge of past generations becomes apparent—those who understood the earth's unspoken wisdom and gifts. The memory is a cherished reminder of nature's might and the urgent need for its preservation for all generations.

My friend, passionate about guavas, often had tiny seeds trapped in his back teeth following his enjoyment of the fruit. Excruciating tooth pain woke him up in the middle of the night. Knowing traditional remedies, his resourceful and wise mother swiftly put a clove on his painful molar. The pain reduced almost immediately, bringing much-needed relief.

People also commonly used plant-based household remedies to treat severe stomachaches. A paste of cumin seeds and onion was the remedy. It was applied to the stomach, and a small amount of cumin seeds also had to be chewed. The solution proved remarkably successful, relieving the pain. Those were some examples showcasing the past successes of plant-based first aid. We're reminded of a time when nature provided straightforward, yet potent cures for everyday health issues.

Halter in Hand

Ancient farming and travel depended significantly on animals. This reminds me of Chickanna, who, in 2005, stood with a halter in his hand at our formation house. His bullock cart was a quaint and unusual sight on the paved roads. Despite its seemingly awkward appearance in modern surroundings, it blended flawlessly with the tranquil ambiance of our property.

Bullock carts, unlike modern vehicles, never had to worry about flat tires. Its "gas tank" was filled with the lush greenery beneath the bullock's feet, providing endless fuel. Sand and rocks were no match for its powerful oxen, the "eight-legged engine," which pulled it with ease.

The cart proved especially helpful in our philosophy house's coconut grove, a place where pepper creeper–adorned trees swayed serenely in the calming breeze. We couldn't have managed the monthly coconut harvest without the bollock cart. It snaked effortlessly through the grove, transporting mature coconuts to the storage shed while the tender ones quenched the thirst of the philosophy students hard at work.

Beyond coconuts, the cart efficiently transported various necessities, including manure, coconut leaves, and firewood. One vivid memory stands out: the day new residents arrived at the formation house. Their luggage was transported from the local bus stand by a cart, doing the job of a modern truck, without any expense. Long-term residents arrived at the house unburdened, the dependable and uncomplicated cart having made their journey easier.

The bullock cart was more than just a vehicle; it was a symbol of resilience, harmony with nature, and a connection to simpler, more sustainable times. The rhythmic movement and peaceful image are unforgettable, symbolizing a life where simple things were beautiful and practical.

Long distances and heavy loads were impossible for humans to manage without the help of animals for transportation. In the past, people relied on animals like oxen, camels, and horses for commuting and other essential tasks. Oxen were essential for ploughing fields, significantly contributing to farming and food production.

In today's world, we cannot afford to forget the invaluable assistance animals have provided throughout history. Human beings ought to show gratitude for their contributions. Although technological breakthroughs, such as the gas engine, revolutionized transport and agriculture, we shouldn't overlook the historical significance of animals in our development.

Humanity still benefits from animals in many ways today. Dogs' remarkable alertness, intelligence, and sense of smell make them invaluable to law enforcement. They are essential for search and rescue, tracking suspects, and detecting contraband. This is why police forces globally depend significantly on K9 units for support.

Humans and animals share a timeless bond, and acknowledging their contributions shows we appreciate and respect nature.

Pet to Companion

James Herriot, a British veterinary surgeon and author, once stated, "I have felt cats rubbing their faces against mine and touching my cheek with claws carefully sheathed. These things, to me, are expressions of love." In this sentiment, he beautifully captures his admiration for the companionship and affection of animals.

It is said that "loneliness kills." Throughout the centuries, people have engaged in the practice of rearing animals. Over time, people began deploying animals, such as dogs, to protect their property. People raised cats for the purpose of keeping mice away. In the present scenario, households keep birds, fish, and other living things as pets. To provide emotional support and as therapy for many individuals, domesticated animals act as companions. In this way what was pets earlier have become companions now.

In *The Power of the Dog*, Rudyard Kipling eloquently depicts the unconditional love of a dog and the emotional toll of such a profound companionship. Among the most touching verses is this one:

> Buy a pup and your money will buy
> Love unflinching that cannot lie—
> Perfect passion and worship fed
> By a kick in the ribs or a pat on the head.
> Nevertheless, it is hardly fair
> To risk your heart for a dog to tear.

A new puppy isn't just an animal; it's a loving, loyal companion you welcome into your home. A dog's love is purely unconditional, unlike human relationships, which can be deceitful and conditional. Its devotion remains steadfast, regardless of how it is treated, whether with kindness ("a pat on the head") or cruelty ("a kick in the ribs"). This showcases the extraordinary selflessness of dog's love, unwavering even amid hardship. However, Kipling also highlights the emotional hazards inherent in such profound connection. The phrase "a dog to tear" suggests the inevitable heartbreak of losing a beloved pet. Despite the immense joy dogs provide, their short life spans inevitably cause sadness. This stanza embodies the bittersweet truth of pet companionship: unconditional love balanced by the certainty of grief. Despite the difficulties, people remain devoted to their dogs due to the unparalleled and deeply fulfilling companionship they provide.

Conclusion

Creation's beauty and harmony reflect the divine wisdom that unites all living things. Just as the womb nurtures new life, flora and fauna envelop and sustain us, providing everything essential for our survival. The beating of our hearts and our very breath depend on oxygen, an often unnoticed gas crucial for survival. Humanity's fundamental needs—food, shelter, and clothing—originate in nature. Plants and animals provide our sustenance, while clothing, initially just protection, showcases our cultural identity, occupation, and mental state. The plant materials in our older shelters reveal our deep dependence on nature. In the same vein, medicine has long been informed by nature's knowledge. For centuries, systems such as Ayurveda and Traditional Chinese Medicine have used nature's resources—plants and animals—to improve human health and well-being. In every respect, our relationship with the natural world is key to human progress and survival.

Similarly, animals that were once valued solely for their utility have become cherished companions, offering emotional support and unconditional affection. Historically, humans have raised animals for protection, pest control, and companionship. Today, pets like dogs, cats, birds, and fish provide comfort and therapeutic value, improving human lives significantly. These are just a few of the benefits we derive from flora and fauna, which contribute to making our lives more comfortable and sustainable

We are responsible for respecting and protecting our environment, recognizing its essential role in nurturing and sustaining life. This sentiment is beautifully captured in *Lumen Fidei No. 55*, where Pope Francis writes,

> Faith, on the other hand, by revealing the love of God the Creator, enables us to respect nature all the more, and to discern in it a grammar written by the hand of God and a dwelling place entrusted to our protection and care. Faith also helps us to devise models of development which are based not simply on utility and profit, but consider creation as a gift for which we are all indebted; it teaches us to create just forms of government, in the realization that authority comes from God and is meant for the service of the common good.

Pope Francis continues,

> Creation's care is entrusted to us, not owned by us. Serving and stewardship are how we'll preserve this divine gift for those who come after us. Cherishing and protecting nature is our responsibility; it's a sacred trust to sustain life and inspire those who follow.

ROLLED IN THEM

I am rolled in them, yet never confined.
They breathe in me the breath of life.
Not cold, not hot, but wrapped so kind
In linen's touch and fur so rife.

I am rolled in them, both full and lean.
They feed me fiber, and feed me fat.
Tied to my feet, through roads unseen,
They bore me forth—on wheels, on back.

Through monsoons and summers, near and far,
They housed me under wooden beams.
With earthen walls and cow-dung floors,
They shaped my nights and wove my dreams.

Weak in sleep, they made me strong,
With roots and eggs, both bitter and sweet.
Lonely days did not last long.
They smiled in flowers, in barks that speak.

I am rolled in them, and now I say,
All I have is born of them.
With grateful heart, in love I stay,
And whisper thanks—forever true.

Chapter 2

Indigenous trust

Indigenous folks globally formed a lasting and intrinsic relationship with flora and fauna. This trust is integral to their civilization and spiritual lives. Indigenous knowledge is formed over the years. It highlights the consistency in living and the interdependence between the human animal-plant worlds. In this chapter, we will explore how indigenous communities trust and interrelate with their natural environments, narrowing on their cultural, ecological, and medicinal aspects of this affiliation. A vast number of indigenous cultures consider nature as sacred and alive. Indigenous cultures perceive ancestral beings or spirits as the creators of the land, plants, and animals. This spiritual framework fosters a deep trust in the natural world and an understanding of humans' role as caretakers rather than dominators.

Reverence is a hallmark of indigenous exchange with flora and fauna. Indigenous customs are intended to safeguard natural life, ensuring its long-term accessibility. Several native communities employ gyratory hunting, fishing, and gathering practices, which enhance the ecosystems, giving them time to recover. Such practices accentuate a trust in the natural world's ability to maintain itself when treated with sensitivity.

The indigenous community's faith in their local plants and animals reveals their extensive understanding and reverence for their world. With the world's significant environmental problems, indigenous cultures' interconnectedness and caretaking offer a model of respectful coexistence with nature. Adopting these principles can help to create a more harmonious and sustainable future for everyone.

In this chapter, we will have a look at the Native American, Indigenous African, and primitive Indian conception of the trust in flora and fauna, noticing how it persuades them to avoid distraction and the extinction of all living things.

America's Life before Discovery

I would like to start this section with Lakota wisdom, which is one of the prominent tribes. "Honor the sacred. Honor the Earth, our Mother. Honor the Elders. Honor all with whom we share the Earth: Four-Leggeds, two-leggeds, winged ones, Swimmers, crawlers, plant and rock people. Walk in balance and beauty." The various First Nations tribal cultures share a common perspective: that all components of nature and the ecosystem are interrelated and have an enormous impact on each other's growth and survival. These inhabitants don't fundamentally believe in becoming superior to fauna and flora. Their inherent respect for nature stems from their belief in its essential role in their survival.

First Nations and Native Americans usually viewed living organisms, including humans, and nature not as distinct creatures. Subsequently, it is obvious for them to perceive the reciprocal affiliation, where humans looked after nature with an expectation that in return nature will take care of humankind. This concept is well framed by Russell Means of the Oglala Lakota Nation. "Before I was six years old, my grandparents and my mother had taught me that if all the green things that grow were taken from the earth, there could be no life. If all the four-legged creatures were taken from the earth, there could be no life. If all the winged creatures were taken from the earth, there could be no life. If all our relatives who crawl and swim and live within the earth were taken away, there could be no life. But if all the human beings were taken away, life on earth would flourish. That is how insignificant we are."

Native Americans didn't recognize the idea of "environment," as they regarded plants, trees, and animals as equal individuals. This explains why the Tree People and the Plant People are among them. They discussed the

Strawberry Sister and the Cedar Sister, and because of this, they showed them reverence.

This respect and love for the land did not prevent Native Americans from taking from nature—they actively hunted vast numbers of buffalo, and reports indicate that some tribes hunted them to extinction in certain areas. The amount and timing of their hunts were, however, influenced by their need. Their broader relationship with nature and ecological consciousness prevented them from overhunting and overfishing species to extinction. They acknowledged the animals' contribution to their livelihood with thanks and respect. Their usual method involved a commitment to maintaining environmental and ecosystem equilibrium. A profound understanding of sustainable practices, many believed, was held by Native Americans.

The idea of land ownership was foreign to various Indigenous North American traditions. While the land was communally owned in their view, tribal disputes over prime hunting grounds and valuable land occasionally occurred. Their actions caused conflict with the people living there, who saw land as something to claim. In the book The Sacred Hoop, Paula Gunn Allen, Laguna Pueblo, put in these words: "We are the land... that is the fundamental idea embedded in Native American life. The Earth is the mind of the people as we are the mind of the earth. The land is not really the place (separate from ourselves) where we act out the drama of our isolate destinies. It is not a means of survival, a setting for our affairs... It is rather a part of our being, dynamic, significant, real. It is our self...

"It is not a matter of being 'close to nature'... The Earth is, in a very real sense, the same as our self (or selves) ...That knowledge, though perfect, does not have associated with it the exalted romance of the sentimental 'nature lovers', nor does it have, at base, any self-conscious 'appreciation' of the land... It is a matter of fact, one known equably from infancy, remembered and honoured at levels of awareness that go beyond consciousness, and that extend long roots into primary levels of mind, language, perception and all the basic aspects of being..." God, in fact, gave land freely to humankind. Human selfishness led to the boundaries that caused property to become fragmented.

Kinship with Flora

We're all familiar with the concept of a family tree. Nevertheless, what if, quite literally, the tree is considered as the part of the family? In this view, plants are more than just a backdrop to our lives; they're our kin, part of our holistic family, and deeply allied to our lives as living beings. The Arapaho Native Americans provide evidence that "all plants are our brothers and sisters. They talk to us and if we listen, we can hear them." The indigenous people integrate flora into the fabric of their cultural, spiritual, and daily routines. For many Native American ethnic groups, the forests are not merely a background to human activity but an integral part of their survival and identity.

Flora is a vital component of the cultural traditions of Native American tribes. Northwest Coast tribes, for example, considered the cedar sacred and crafted totem poles and masks from it. For Ojibwe tribes and others, birch bark was essential in crafting household items, canoes, and baskets.

Spiritual ceremonies also heavily relied on plants. Lakota and other Plains tribes used sage, sweet grass, and cedar for smudging ceremonies to purify and protect areas. The ceremonial smoking of sacred plants, like tobacco, in pipes also demonstrates their cultural impact. These customs are deeply meaningful, connecting us to the spiritual realm while honoring Mother Earth.

The acquaintance with medicinal plants is a phenomenal characteristic of Native American tradition. Native Americans had discovered sophisticated categorization of herbal medicine, using plants to treat a variety of sicknesses long before modern medicine. The Cherokee, for instance, used black cohosh for gynecological concerns and goldenrod for respiratory issues. The Navajo and Apache used yucca root as shampoo for treating dandruff and hair loss.

Several tribes believe in the idea of animism, where they embrace all the rudiments of nature, so they perceive plants and trees as possessing a spirit. This conviction fosters a profound respect and awakens the spark of responsibility toward the planet.

Among some of the tribes, there is the concept of the vision quest, a traditional rite for numerous tribes akin to initiation. The vision quest involves embarking on a solitary journey into the wilderness to seek personal development and spiritual guidance from the spirits within certain Native American cultures. Young males entering adulthood normally undertook this quest. Sacred trees, like the cottonwood used in the Lakota sun dance, powerfully symbolize life, growth, and connection to the Creator.

Here are some important examples of how Native Americans and indigenous people showed love and respect for plants and trees: They would always have the feeling of being in debt to the magnanimity of the flora. This life experience of theirs moved them to protect flora. This kind of sentiment led them to selective harvesting, not clear-cutting. In this way, they enhanced the growth and rejuvenation of the forest. For example, they would use only the mature trees and neglect the younger ones to maintain production. For gathering and harvesting, people employed a system of rotating land use across various patches. This enriched land and allowed it to recover and restore before being used again.

Tribes like Karuk, Yurok, and Pomo practiced the intelligent method of controlled burns to handle forest ecosystems. By clearing underbrush and promoting fire-adapted plants, these controlled burns successfully mitigated wildfire risks. It also helped in preserving open spaces that were helpful for hunting and the growth of certain plants.

Indigenous people held certain trees and groves sacred, shielding them from harm and logging. These areas held spiritual significance, so people refrained from disturbing or harvesting them. Sacred or cultural ceremonies made use of particular species or individual trees, extending the concept of holiness to them.

Here I would like to write about the "Three Sisters" method, a type of companion planting involving corn, beans, and squash. This technique improved soil fertility, reduced pests, and increased the yield without reducing the fertility of the land.

Native Americans also practiced agroforestry, which involves incorporating trees into agricultural lands. This preserved biodiversity and ensured tree cover. The area's rich topsoil and partial shade, from the nearby trees, allowed them to cultivate a large vegetable garden with ease during the hottest time of day.

Respectful nature ceremonies and practices led to better preservation of plant and tree populations. They performed prayers before harvesting to honor the spirit of the tree and ensure that they only took the necessary quantities, leaving behind greed. Many stories in the Salish oral tradition tell of medicine trees whose spirits provided protection, visions, and gifts. People regarded these trees as shrines where they would place offerings and seek spiritual guidance. The native communities handled natural resources management. Equal resource distribution and the prevention of overexploitation were ensured within the community.

Fauna Sacrificed yet Conserved

We'll quickly cover how Native Americans interacted with animals in this section. In Native American customs, animals were used to convey the morals and spiritual beliefs of the societies. Animals' significance is also noticeable in the creation stories of several tribes. They painted animal images to share family, clan, and personal stories. Cherokee narratives and traditions, for instance, stress the value of each animal and plant, thereby reinforcing the concept of humans as an integral, yet not singular, part of nature. They had also introduced the kinship system among various American Indian tribal groups to reflect relationships with animals. Each animal signifies the history and importance.

We are told that fauna was the crucial part of native folks' livelihoods. They hunted animals but not a single part would go to waste. For instance, native peoples made tools and weapons from the animal's bones, and its hide became clothing, teepees, and blankets. People treated every animal with respect and recognized that each animal had a physical or spiritual purpose. However, the treatment of the fauna differed from tribe to tribe. Despite widespread respect for animals among tribes, some tribesmen killed them to show their community their bravery and adulthood, not for food. It was a ritual to kill wolves and bears. Some tribes wore its skin to prove they were worthy of being a warrior. The ritual seems cruel to us because it wasn't for a feast, even though they certainly used the hunted animal entirely. Some of the other tribes were against killing sacred animals, such as wolves, bears, and mountain lions.

We also learned from various sources that many Native American cultures showed great respect for animals. As an example, some Native American tribes customarily offered prayers of gratitude to the animal before it was consumed. In this way, they gave thanks for the life and the nourishment it offered. This ensured their relationship with nature remained harmonious. This practice also demonstrates a spiritual link with nature, acknowledging the sacredness of all living things. It doesn't seem only fair but it's a basic rule of this earth that for one animal to sustain another has to lay down its life. Here, thanking the animal for its life-giving sacrifice is completely understandable.

Though the Native Americans used fauna for many purposes, they also protected it. Now let us see the steps they took to protect the animals. They engaged in seasonal and selective hunting practices. They implemented seasonal hunting restrictions to prevent interference with breeding. This would enhance the animal population. The animals hunted were chosen carefully, leaving younger and breeding females to maintain the population.

The region's resources weren't overexploited due to regulated hunting, which helped animal populations recover. The sacred areas were off-limits for hunting and fishing. This let animals thrive undisturbed.

Some tribes had ethical and cultural codes that had particular taboos against killing certain animals. Those animals had a spiritual significance. Another fact was the hunted animal was to be used in its best way possible. Oral traditions and collective decisions were also popular among most tribes. Oral tradition enabled the tribes to pass on knowledge of animal behavior, migration patterns, and environmental resources. This wealth of information allowed them to make decisions about resource management and animal protection. The hunting was the venture of the community. As a result, there was control over killing animals.

As a conclusion, native people felt the duty and responsibility to pass on the knowledge to future generations. It's not just a matter of preserving resources or practicing austerity but of ensuring that the legacy they left behind was one of care and growth. We are all interconnected with everything else on the planet. Like annual blooms nurtured by a higher power, we should nurture and protect those around us.

Consider nature's cycles: What blooms today will return, nurtured by the earth. Considering the Creator's focus on plants and trees, our responsibility to each other and the planet as stewards should be even greater. We've been given this planet by the Creator; therefore, it's our responsibility to take good care of it. As my grandfather used to say, we must protect the planet and each other so future generations can thrive.

Africa's Ancient Inhabitant

When we think of African inhabitants, the gazillion rituals come to our mind. Although African regions vary in their interpretations and practices, they share a common bond with community, nature, and spirituality. They believe spirits dwell in the sacred objects and places. This understanding also gives rise to the fact of totems in African ontology. For sure, belief in totems is a reality among African flocks. The African flocks consider particular animals, trees, places, and individuals as totems. The people perceive them as objects that symbolize something factual and enhance such beliefs. Furthermore, people believe that totems have some supernatural and spiritual powers. In most African tribes, it is a taboo and a violation of cultural and spiritual aspect to kill a totemic animal or plant. People handle totems with the utmost care and respect.

Warm Forest

I call it a warm forest because a living body is warm compared to the coldness of a lifeless one. To the ancient African inhabitants, the forest was warm, animated, and alive. Here let us explore how Africans traditionally show respect for plants. The African cosmological view of reality is indivisible from the African understanding of the forest. They perceive life as an incorporated bond and interconnected web. There is no definite and absolute dualism in the native African worldview. All life spirits, humans, animals, plants, trees, oceans, rocks, etc., come from God. They rely on the Creator, God, for their existence and sustenance. In the native African worldview, the Creator facilitates active and dynamic life in all living beings.

Let's use the baobab tree as an example to improve our understanding. Across Africa, the baobab tree is revered and known as the "Tree of Life." Its three-hundred-plus life-sustaining applications highlight its deep connection between humanity and nature. The tree offers numerous healing properties in its fruits, leaves, and bark, supporting community sustenance and well-being. The baobab holds deep cultural significance, fueled by myths, legends, and spiritual beliefs. The baobab's hardiness in harsh conditions makes it a symbol of resilience and strength, powerfully representing survival and perseverance. As a symbol of resilience, the baobab provides sustenance and inspiration to its caretakers amid times of change and transformation.

The African conception recognizes that the consciousness found within human beings is also present in trees, emphasizing the need to treat them with equal respect and care. It highlights the importance of treating trees with the same respect and care as we treat ourselves. This approach not only prevents harm but also serves as an environmental protection method. When harvesting parts of a tree, it becomes crucial to avoid cutting down the entire tree, ensuring its availability for future generations and others who may need it. Acknowledging and appreciating the tree is essential.

In African metaphysical ontology, the forests derive their intrinsic value from their pantheistic-psychic base, which implies that the divine dynamic force and spirit of the Creator permeates all creation. It is this that gives value to all things, not simply their utility.

Native African communities have historically used the surrounding fauna in various ways, deeply integrating it into their cultures, economies, and daily lives.

Here are some significant ways in which native African communities have used flora: They prevented cut down or harm to the trees and plants that were associated with deities, ancestors, or the spirits. This was because of their spiritual significance. Bringing down such trees was taboo. The slash-and-burn agriculture practice facilitated them to restore the fertility of the fields. Not using the land for a certain duration would enable it to regain its productivity. Sustainable harvesting styles applied to medicinal plants assured their availability for future generations. Earlier generations passed down information about these practices. The traditional African communities engaged in planting trees to retain degraded lands and ensured a regular supply of resources, such as firewood, fruits, and medicinal plants. Integrating trees and shrubs into agricultural systems helped to maintain plant biodiversity, improve soil productiveness, and provide shade and protection for crops. Cultural ceremonies and oral traditions often emphasized reverence for nature and the interconnectedness of all life forms. Stories and songs were used to pass down the wealth of knowledge about plants and their conservation methods, ensuring that the next generation understood the value of flora. Sharing resources within the community and establishing guidelines for resources, assisted to manage and protect plant life.

The Lion King

The title *The Lion King* is inspired by the movie of the same name, which many of us have watched. Set amid the African wilderness, the movie delves into leadership, community, and the circle of life, mirroring ancient African spiritual concepts. In African culture, lions have long been powerful symbols of strength, courage, and protection. In many cultures, lions symbolize protection, authority, and power over the land. In addition to their physical strength, lions hold symbolic roles as guides, leaders, and sacred figures in various myths, stories, and spiritual practices. This essence is beautifully depicted in *The Lion King*, which celebrates the strong connection between nature, leadership, and the balance of life—as the lion represents these in ancient African cultures.

    The ancient African societies demonstrated a profound respect for animals, which was reflected in their cultural practices, religious beliefs, and daily lives. Ancient African societies showcased respect for animals in various aspects, such as their art, mythology, and sustainable use of natural resources. Many ancient African cultures practiced animism, the belief that animals and inanimate objects possess a spiritual essence. Many ancient African cultures often considered animals sacred and believed that they possessed unique spiritual qualities. This belief system fostered a deep respect for animals as integral parts of the natural and spiritual world. In many African religions, deities were associated with certain animals. For example, in ancient Egyptian mythology, numerous gods and goddesses were depicted with animal forms or heads. The representation of Bastet, the goddess of home and fertility, as a lioness or a woman with a lioness's head highlights the sacredness of lions. African art often depicted animals with great detail and reverence, symbolizing their importance in the natural and spiritual realms. Rock paintings, sculptures, and masks frequently featured animals, reflecting their roles in myths, rituals, and daily life. The San people of southern Africa have a rich tradition of rock art depicting animals, which reflects their intimate relationship with the natural world. Their traditional practices are based on a deep understanding of animal behavior and ecology, highlighting a harmonious coexistence with wildlife.

For the Maasai people of east Africa, cattle are not only a primary source of sustenance but also hold deep cultural and spiritual significance. The Maasai people believe cattle are a gift from the gods and closely connect their welfare to the well-being of the community.

African folktales and proverbs frequently feature animals as central characters, embodying moral lessons and cultural values. Stories of cunning hares, wise tortoises, and noble lions are abundant, illustrating the traits admired and respected by the society.

Traditional ecological knowledge, passed down through generations, emphasized sustainable use and conservation of wildlife. Many African societies implemented taboos and customs that prevented overhunting and promoted the protection of certain species during breeding seasons.

Animal hides and skins, such as those from cattle, goats, and wild game, were used to make clothing, footwear, and shelters. Tanners and artisans processed these materials through tanning and other techniques to make them durable and suitable for various uses. They used feathers and fur for decorative purposes and to make blankets, hats, and other clothing items, providing warmth and comfort. People fashioned animal bones and horns into tools, weapons, utensils, and musical instruments. For example, horns could create containers or musical instruments like the kudu horn. Ancient African civilizations used shells from marine animals as tools, ornaments, and, in some cases, as currency.

Traditional medicine practitioners used various parts of animals, including fats, organs, and bones. People used certain animal products in remedies and treatments because they believed they had healing properties. They raised livestock, such as cattle, goats, and sheep, for meat, milk, and hides. Cattle, in particular, served as a means of ploughing fields and were a symbol of wealth and social status in many African societies. Animal dung served as fertilizer to enrich soil for crop production and a fuel source for cooking and heating.

In spite of using animals for their numerous needs, the native African communities have historically employed various measures to protect and conserve fauna, ensuring the sustainability of their natural resources and maintaining ecological balance. Often, native African communities rooted these measures in traditional knowledge, cultural practices, and spiritual beliefs. Some key conservation practices include the following:

Many communities practiced seasonal hunting, allowing animals to reproduce and grow during certain times of the year. This prevented overhunting and ensured a steady supply of game. To maintain healthy populations, hunters often followed guidelines on which animals they could hunt, typically avoiding young, breeding, or endangered species. People set aside and protected certain areas of land, known as sacred groves, for religious or spiritual reasons. These areas provided refuge for wildlife by prohibiting hunting and deforestation. Resource supervision was often a communal effort, with local leaders and councils establishing rules and monitoring the use of natural resources. Local leaders and councils ensured the sustainable use of wildlife through community control. Communities had well-defined territorial boundaries, and respect for these boundaries helped in managing and protecting wildlife habitats effectively.

These traditional conservation measures reflect a deep understanding of the environment and a holistic approach to managing natural resources. By integrating cultural, spiritual, and practical knowledge, native African communities could live in harmony with their natural surroundings and protect flora for future generations.

In conclusion, the respect for animals and plants in ancient African societies was deeply ingrained in their spiritual viewpoint, cultural practices, and ecological acquaintance. This reverence ensured a balanced and respectful relationship with the natural world, which has continued to influence contemporary attitudes toward wildlife and vegetative conservation in Africa.

Vedic Period

In ancient India, the Vedic period is when the Vedas, Hinduism's oldest sacred texts, were written. This period, approximately 1500 BCE to 500 BCE, was crucial in establishing the spiritual, cultural, and societal base of Indian civilization. Its lifestyle revolved around rituals, hymns, and prayers dedicated to natural forces and gods, such as Agni, Indra, and Surya. In Vedic times, agrarian life dominated society and was characterized by a profound respect for nature and the cosmic order. The Vedas provided a foundation for philosophical exploration, which later led to concepts like karma, dharma, and moksha. This time is a high point for knowledge, spirituality, and cultural development.

In Vedic times, there was profound respect for animals and plants, rooted in the belief that all forms of life were interconnected and sacred. The Vedas, ancient Hindu scriptures, emphasized living in harmony with nature and considering it a divine manifestation. Animals were revered not only for their utility but also for their spiritual significance, with many being associated with deities, such as the cow, regarded as a symbol of abundance and motherhood. Plants, too, were held in high esteem, with sacred trees, like the Peepal and Tulsi, being worshipped for their life-sustaining properties. Rituals often included offerings of fruits, flowers, and grains to honor nature, while hymns expressed gratitude for the bountiful gifts. This deep respect fostered a culture of conservation, ensuring that natural resources were used sustainably and with reverence.

Tree Worship

Indians have revered trees for many centuries. They strongly believe the Creator made trees to nourish and sustain life in various ways. Ancient belief held that cutting flora was sinful, as people treated them like sons. Since Vedic times, the worship of trees has been the most common and basic form of religious practice. Divinity, residing within trees, received its due recognition from people. As a result, they axed them harmoniously suitable only for their needs and not to fulfill their greed. The well-being of trees was envisioned by ancient Indian sages, who described their divine and medicinal qualities. Trees have long been admired in the rich body of Indian literature.

Let's consider few conceptions about the trees. According to Sage Vyasa's *Mahabharata*, trees are conscious beings that react to heat, cold, and thunder. The statement claims that plants have hearing capabilities similar to humans.

The *Varaha Purana* 162.41–42 articulates that trees offer five significant favors akin to five grand sacrifices (*Panchayajna*): fuel for inheritance, shade for shelter, resting spots for travelers, nesting places for birds, and medicinal resources from bark, roots, and leaves.

To enhance family, wealth, and future happiness, the *Agni Purana Varuna Aramapratishtha* advises against cutting down trees that bear good flowers and fruits. Lord Yama's agents, in Asipatra's grim, sword-leaved forests, torment the man who cut down the cool shade trees.

In post-Vedic texts, ancient Indians held trees in high regard, going as far as celebrating the marriages of specific tree species to maintain a harmonious ecological balance. It's seen as an insect because its pollination is like a marriage between the plant's male and female parts, producing fruit.

The Vedas, Upanishads, and Puranas, ancient texts, stress the value of trees and forests. For example, Ashoka's edict encouraged tree planting and the creation of groves. Events such as Van Mahotsav and rituals related to tree worship promote the protection of trees. Educators instilled in their pupils the significance of trees and forests, cultivating a culture of care and preservation. Forests supplied essential resources, such as fuel wood, fodder, and medicinal plants. Sustainable use and protection of local forests were ensured through collective community management. Specifically, village councils (Panchayats) participated in forest management, including rule enforcement and conflict resolution regarding forest use. Check dams, ponds, and step wells were built to supply water to forests, prevent soil erosion, and protect trees. This is how the Indian natives took care of plants.

Vehicle of Gods

I titled this because, unlike any other civilization, only in Indian traditions do we find animals revered as the vehicles of gods. This unique feature underscores the deep link between nature and spirituality within Indian culture. Animals like Shiva's Nandi (cow), Vishnu's Garuda(Eagle), and Ganesha's mouse are more than just symbols; their qualities, such as strength, loyalty, agility, and devotion, perfectly match the gods they serve. This viewpoint portrays a unified world where animals hold sacred status, acting as vital links between humanity and the spiritual world within a divine framework.

In ancient India, animals held a revered status, often seen as either deities themselves or as the vehicles of deities. Vehicles, or vahanas, were deeply symbolic and philosophically important. They were often depicted in classical Indian literature and art, representing both real and mythological forms. These vahanas often symbolized negative traits conquered by the deities they carried, or positive traits humans should aspire to. For example, Lord Kartikeya, pictured riding a peacock—a symbol of beauty and pride—symbolizes triumph over vanity and arrogance. These portrayals highlight the significant spiritual and moral importance of animals within Indian culture, demonstrating their function as not only symbols but also as instructors and guides within the cosmic scheme.

Animals were often featured in myth creation in the Indian Hindu tradition, such as in the Ramayana and Mahabharata and the Samudra Manthana, where they played a vital role in illuminating the battle between good and evil.

The concept of *ahimsa* (nonviolence) in Jain, Buddhist, and certain Hindu sects strongly advocates the well-being of all living creates, which includes the absolute prohibition of the consumption of meat. This principle not only enhances the coexistence of fauna with humans but also the protection of the animal world as seen in the image of Krishna with the cows and Gopis.

Animals were depicted as royal insignia owing to their virility and magnificent appearance. The National Emblem of India in 1950, featuring a monolithic column with four lions facing the four cardinal directions, was created by King Ashoka's during the Maurya Dynasty in the fourth and second centuries BCE.

If we read about the history of animals, human companionship, or even coexistence, we will notice for most countries, this love for fauna is comparatively recent. While most countries have realized the value of animals recently, India had been off the trend in this regard and has forever been an advocator of animal care. India is a country that has animal care embedded in its culture. Let me end this with the quote by Dr. Kumud Kanitkar, who has conducted an exhaustive study of animal sculptures and design in Indian culture. He says, "The Romans saw animals as fierce creatures which had to be killed or controlled for human survival. The Greeks saw them as symbols of power living in a separate world of their own. But ancient Indians saw them as they should be seen—friendly, loyal and graceful."

Conclusion

Throughout history, numerous ancient traditions across diverse cultures have emphasized the well-being of flora and fauna. Here, we have highlighted only three such traditions, but many more exist, each rooted in deep respect for the natural world. Our forefathers regarded flora and fauna as profound mysteries. Filled with awe and reverence, they honored the natural world and all the creatures within it. Their deep respect for nature is echoed in the words of Chief Dan George of the Tsleil-Waututh Nation (1899–1981), who wisely stated, "If you talk to the animals, they will talk with you, and you will know each other. If you do not talk to them, you will not know them, and what you do not know, you will fear. What one fears, one destroys." In this quote, he emphasizes the importance of understanding and respecting animals, suggesting that a lack of connection with nature leads to fear and, ultimately, destruction.

Ancient civilizations, even without modern science, recognized the intricate relationship between flora and fauna through keen observation. The wisdom of this connection is captured in the *Rig Veda*, an ancient Hindu text, which advises, "Do not trouble trees. Do not uproot or cut them. They provide protection to animals, birds, and other living beings." This profound insight highlights the ecological interdependence of all living things andurgeshumans to protect nature as a means of sustaining life itself.

ONE AND OTHER

They were born together—one and other,
Human and creature, bound like no other.

One with reason, the other with drive,
One with wisdom, the other naive.

One placed a hand on the other's side,
To lead the way, to guard, to guide.

The other followed, silent and true,
Asking for nothing yet giving its due.

With insight, one held reverence deep,
While the other gave with nothing to keep.

The one, a nomad, roamed for meat and grain,
The other stayed, offering all without gain.

Together they walked, their fates split,
One with a soul, the other with just spirit.

Chapter 3

Nurturing Nerves

As nerves help to supply blood to the entire body, so the flora and fauna together pump life in the ecosystem. Flora and fauna reciprocally nurture each other, serving as the spring of life for the entire universe. Just as nerves connect different parts of the body and are responsible for sensations within them, similarly, plants and animals depend on each other. The interdependent DNA of plants and animals creates equilibrium, exemplifying life within ecosystems. If there accrues imbalance in one, this can lead to natural hazards. There is a profound lesson to be learned from flora and fauna about how they assist in each other's growth. The interdependence is beautifully illustrated in Emily Dickinson's poem "A Bird Came Down the Walk."

Opening the poem is a detailed, intimate scene of a bird, oblivious to the poet, performing its natural actions.

> A Bird, came down the Walk -
> He did not know I saw -
> He bit an Angle Worm in halves
> And ate the fellow, raw,
>
> And then, he drank a Dew
> From a convenient Grass -
> And then hopped sidewise to the Wall
> To let a Beetle pass -

At first, the scene appears peaceful as the bird moves along a path, creating a sense of quiet curiosity. However, the bird's tranquility is short-lived; it instinctively snaps an angleworm in half and devours it raw. The current situation emphasizes nature's unfiltered and sometimes brutal truth, showing how survival is integral to its beauty. Here, we see that animals and plants depend on each other—even in ways that may seem harsh.

As the bird sips dew, the poem adopts a gentler tone, showcasing its elegance. This imagery emphasizes nature's harmonious balance of destruction and renewal. The bird's next action—hopping sideways to allow a beetle to pass—further reinforces this sense of natural order. The bird's predatory instincts don't lead to needless killing, unlike human behavior which often involves excessive resource exploitation and storage. This subtle observation underlines the wisdom of the natural world, where creatures take only what they need.

The complexity and independence of nature, untouched by humanity, are captured by Dickinson's juxtaposition of contrasting images—violence with delicacy, movement with stillness. The poet uses simple yet striking images to lead the reader to consider nature's seamless blend of elegance and survival.

We began by exploring, in the first chapter, the deep impact of flora and fauna on humanity, detailing their importance in providing food, oxygen, medicine, and maintaining ecological equilibrium. We now turn our attention to the vital relationships between flora and fauna that sustain ecosystems. Plants, the primary producers, use solar energy to start the food web; animals help plants grow and spread through pollination, seed dispersal, and nutrient cycling. This interdependent relationship encourages biodiversity, stabilizes habitats, and preserves the delicate balance essential for life's flourishing. Plants and animals together show how vital mutual support is for healthy ecosystems and the planet.

Nest and Rest

What I have done! These were the words of my niece after the departure of Bulbul from its nest. On a sunny summer day, my niece, while hunting for the wild berries, discovered the nest of a bulbul bird. She was on cloud nine when she learned that it was occupied by three white eggs with brown spots. She felt pity for the fragile eggs and brought them down. Her pure intention was of protecting the future chicks, and she covered the spiky straw with cotton. Her girly nature couldn't stop her from adorning the nest with flowers.

After her adventures and compassionate act, she waited with opened eyes to see the mother bulbul. After a ten-minute wait, the bird arrived. Mother failed to recognize the nest and panic engulfed her with the sorrow in her chirping. She never returned. My niece's innocent gesture slipped into a dungeon of guilt. On that day she learned a lesson for her life and never dared to play with nature again. Numerous birds' species make their nest to lay egg in the trees. The trees provide elevated places for birds to build their nests, which enables them to shield their eggs and young ones from predators. Nature knows to nurture and care, and sometimes artificial comforts by human can be troublesome.

Birds use a variety of materials to construct their nests, such as twigs, leaves, grasses, feathers, and even mud. The kind of nest and the materials used can vary greatly between different bird species. Here are some of the examples: Robins and sparrows usually engineer cup-shaped nests using grass, twigs, and feathers. Woodpeckers are known for their strong beaks, which assists them in carving out cavities in tree trunks to create nests. The high-altitude flying eagle builds large nests, called aeries, high up in tall trees, fixing sticks and even wires. Weaver birds are masters of engineering and build chic woven nests using grasses and fibers, often hanging from tree branches, especially palm trees. All this takes place because of preordained calculating from nature. If anybody attempts to interfere, it can backfire.

On that day John had a barrel of laughter. What was the fault of the camouflaged white caterpillar on the gray branch of Guava tree? It was innocent, yet Toney was afraid. It was afternoon. Toney's mother would not allow him to go play outside on a scorching summer's day. She commanded them to have a nap beside her. Most of the time he and his brother John pretended to be sleeping. As soon as Mother was in deep slumber, they would take off from home. On that day Toney, with great excitement, climbed the guava tree. Before he could come down, he encountered a big caterpillar with white spiky hair. That led to teasing by John. His shouting woke their mother from sleep, and she came holding tight a stick to beat them for not listening. Now it was John's turn to mock for Toney always got scared of caterpillars. With that he jumped from three feet above.

The tree was inhabited by caterpillars. It was where it supposed to be, and Toney was where he was not supposed to be. Some animals make their homes on plants without causing any harm. For instance, large number of insects, birds, and tiny mammal's dwell in trees and shrubs. Epiphytes, like orchids and bromeliads, host different insects and frogs.

Birds of the sky rest on the branches of the trees. It is evident when we visit the woods in the morning that we hear the chirping of the birds. You will not hear that in between the skyscrapers downtown.

To summarize our discussion of the animal-plant relationship, consider William Wordsworth's "The Sparrow's Nest."

> BEHOLD, within the leafy shade,
> Those bright blue eggs together laid!
> On me the chance-discovered sight
> Gleamed like a vision of delight.
> I started—seeming to espy
> The home and sheltered bed,
> The Sparrow's dwelling, which, hard by
> My Father's house, in wet or dry,
> My sister Emmeline and I
> Together visited.

Wordsworth's poem depicts a child's profound discovery of a sparrow's nest hidden in the leaves. Themes of nature's nurturing, childhood wonder, and family are prominent in this passage.

Beginning with the command, "Behold, within the leafy shade," the poem highlights the nest's hidden, sheltered location. The phrase "leafy shade" implies a secure, protective setting, echoing the belief that nature safeguards its inhabitants. This sense of protection mirrors the role of flora in sustaining fauna.

A striking visual of "bright blue eggs laid together" emphasizes the beauty and fragility of new life. Purity, hope, and future promise are often represented by the color blue, which underscores innocence and renewal. Here, the eggs stand for the life cycle, emphasizing nature's delicate balance and interdependence.

Wordsworth's phrase "gleamed like a vision of delight" conveys a sense of awe and wonder. The luminosity and magic suggested by "gleamed" elevates the nest's discovery beyond a physical event to a spiritual one. This is consistent with the Romantic notion that nature can evoke intense feelings and self-examination.

Additionally, the reference to Wordsworth's sister, Emmeline, underscores the relationship between nature and human relationships. Visiting a sparrow's nest together shows how nature builds family bonds and creates childhood memories. Humans, animals, and plants living together peacefully highlights the poem's message of natural harmony.

Wordsworth uses "The Sparrow's Nest" to showcase nature's nurturing effect and the delicate balance between plants and animals. This poem is a fitting end to our conversation; it shows that nature provides beauty, shelter, and inspiration in addition to sustenance.

Kiss of love

The kiss of love reminds me about the metaphysical poem "The Flea" by John Donne.

> Mark but this flea, and mark in this,
> How little that which thou deniest me is;
> It sucked me first, and now sucks thee,
> And in this flea our two bloods mingled be;
> Thou know'st that this cannot be said
> A sin, nor shame, nor loss of maidenhead,
> Yet this enjoys before it woo,
> And pampered swells with one blood made of two,
> And this, alas, is more than we would do.

The point I like to take from this poem is the union of blood. For the flea, he says, has sucked first his blood and then his beloved's blood so that now, inside the flea, they are mingled and that union cannot be called "sin, or shame, or loss of maidenhead." The flea has joined them together in a way that "alas, is more than we would do." As his beloved intends to kill the flea, the speaker rebukes her, requesting her to spare the three lives in the flea: his life, her life, and the flea's own life. For the benefit of our theme, I would consider the bite of the flea as the kiss of love for according to the poet, that act of the flea mingles the blood of lover and the beloved. In this section we will see how fauna assist flora to multiply.

The kiss of a bee infuses love in the flower. The kiss of the bird or animal to a fruit, the fall of seeds enables life in the ground. Insignificant fauna, such as bees, butterflies, birds, and mammals, play vital roles in pollinating flowers. Pollination is crucial for the reproduction of flowering plants, allowing them to produce seeds and fruits. In pollination the pollen is transferred from the male part of a flower (anther) to the female part of a flower (stigma). This plays significant role in the reproduction of flowering plants. Pollination can occur through various means. In turn, these fruits and seeds support the continuity and dispersal of plant species. Here the tiny creatures become responsible for small and big fruits. Numerous flora plays a role in dispersing seeds of plants. This can happen through various means, such as ingestion (animals consume fruits and disperse seeds through their droppings), attachment (seeds sticking to fur or feathers), or carrying (animals transport seeds to new area). Seed dispersal helps plants inhabit new areas and increase their size.

These creatures are not aware of the impact they create in the ecosystems. Though their act seems to be trivial, it is a crucial one. Pollination leads to fertilization, where the pollen fertilizes the ovule, leading to the formation of seeds and fruit. It's essential for the production of many crops and maintaining biodiversity in ecosystems.

To conclude this subtopic, I'd like to share a moral lesson learned from observing squirrels. Though squirrels are said to bury thousands of nuts and seeds each year, they reportedly forget the locations of up to 74 percent of them! These forgotten seeds sprout into trees, contributing to the growth of forests and reforestation. Some of the world's most ancient forests have expanded thanks to these tiny creatures. The dispersal of oak, hickory, and pine trees, vital for biodiversity and cleaner air, depends significantly on squirrels.

Next time you see a squirrel scurrying around, remember that they're not just adorable; they're accidental ecowarriors.

The moral we can draw from the squirrel's actions is that, just as the squirrel forgets about the nuts it buries, we too should forget the good deeds we perform. We should act selflessly, without expecting anything in return. Real kindness means giving freely, without desire for praise or reward. And as the seed that was hidden by a squirrel one day becomes an enormous tree, in the same way, our good act will grow and bring prosperity in others' lives.

Least Ones Feasting

Let me start with a quote from *Bringing a Garden to Life* (1998) by Carol Williams: "An agricultural adage says the tiny animals that live below the surface of a healthy pasture weigh more than the cows grazing above it. In a catalogue selling composting equipment, I read that two handfuls of healthy soil contain more living organisms than there are people on the Earth. What these beings are and what they can be doing is difficult to even begin to comprehend, but it helps to realize that even though they are many, they work as one." In this passage, Williams highlights the insightful interconnectedness of life, stressing that even the smallest organisms play a crucial role in maintaining the integrity of nature. Their collective efforts sustain the delicate balance of ecosystems, demonstrating that every living being, no matter how tiny, contributes to the greater whole.

Least ones feasting is the total dependence of least living organism on flora. Plants generate microhabitats with unique environmental conditions that support specialized fauna. The trees age and fall. These fallen logs create a favorable environment teeming with life. Decaying lumber provides a dwelling for fungi, insects, and small animals, which in turn, add to nutrient cycling and soil configuration. Thick plant growth and dense vegetation generates moist and dappled atmospheres that are ideal for diverse organism and insects to breed. These umbrellas of foliage offer protection and shelter from predators and harsh weather conditions, respectively.

Pasture into Prey

The theme *pasture into prey* speaks to the cycle of life, where each stage of being transitions into another—sometimes in harmony, sometimes in inevitable sacrifice. Consider this example for better understanding:

Plea of a Hen! Many moons ago, in the heart of a quaint Goan village, nearly every household nurtured a brood of hens, their gentle clucks blending harmoniously with the morning breeze. More than a food source, these feathered animals symbolized the richness of the countryside. Should an egg produce a rooster, its lifespan was limited, ending at the next big feast. But if the egg bore a hen, she was cherished, nurtured, and raised for her golden-yolked, organic treasures.

With the sunrise, the hens were let loose across the homestead, and the dew-kissed grass welcomed them. A small portion of wheat or leftover rice, their simple breakfast, was scattered before them like a blessing. For the rest of the day, they kept themselves occupied by searching the ground for grass and insects, a meal provided by nature.

Yet, their freedom was not without peril. Ever alert, the owners paid close attention to their hens' desperate pleas. The first plea of distress would come when the cunning fox slinked into the village, its amber eyes gleaming with hunger. I recall how my mother, who was wise and forward-thinking, came up with a clever solution by trimming the tail feathers of our hens. Long, fluttering tail feathers were advantageous for the prowling foxes in catching the hen.

But the second plea—oh the second was one of sheer terror! The mother hen shielded her new chicks under her wings when the hawk's shadow, a sign of danger, fell on the land. A frantic warning call alerted them to stay hidden; the circling predator above waited for any mistake. The earth and sky's ancient conflict is a timeless chase between predator and prey.

Beneath the warm Goan sun, the hens existed in a delicate yet strong manner, both nurtured and threatened, their plea-filled voices creating a song of survival that resonated throughout the village.

Here we see the profound truth of *pasture into prey*. The wheat and rice, once mere grains that came from flora, were transformed into the flesh of the hen. In turn, the hen became prey for others. A never-ending cycle, the food chain, nourishes life; each being plays a role in nature's balance.

Many animals rely directly on plants for food. Herbivores feed on leaves, fruits, seeds, and flowers of various plants. These plants provide essential nutrients and energy for their survival and growth. Flora serves diets of many huge animals, becoming the primary food source. The herbivores become the prey for the carnivorous animals

Herbivores are animals that survive exclusively on plant and vegetation. They can be found in a variety of environments, from vast grasslands to dense forests. Here are some prominent examples: Grazers, these animals mainly feed on grass for instance cows, sheep, and horses. Browsers are the animals that make leaves, twigs, and high-growing vegetation their livelihood. Deer and giraffes are the best example in this category. Frugivores are those birds and primates whose diet is principally fruit. Granivores are those creatures who feed on seeds; sparrows and rodents are some of the example. These herbivores are adapted to digest plant material efficiently. For instance, ruminants, like cows, have specific stomachs with multiple chambers to break down tough plant fibers.

Carnivores are animals that prey on herbivores, producing an essential link in the food chain. Predators, like lions, hyenas, and eagles, depend on herbivores for their nutritional needs. This voracious relationship helps maintain ecological balance by controlling herbivore populations, preventing overgrazing, and promoting biodiversity.

The Circle of Life is the interaction between plants, herbivores, and carnivores, which crafts a balanced circle in natural world. This intricate web of interaction ensures the constancy of ecosystems. Plants are the principal producers. Through the process of photosynthesis, they convert sunlight into energy. Herbivores are the chief consumers of vegetation, transferring energy to higher levels. Carnivores are the secondary consumers, regulating herbivore populations and maintaining ecosystem health. This life circle is so well designed but self-interference of humans can cause chaos.

Let us conclude with a fitting passage from Psalm 104:14–21.

> You cause the grass to grow for the cattle,
> and plants for people to cultivate,
> bringing forth food from the earth—
> wine to gladden the human heart,

oil to make the face shine,
and bread to strengthen the human heart.
The trees of the LORD are watered abundantly,
the cedars of Lebanon that He planted.
In them the birds build their nests;
the stork has its home in the fir trees.
The high mountains are for the wild goats;
the rocks are a refuge for the coneys.
You made the moon to mark the seasons;
the sun knows it's time for setting.
You bring darkness, and it is night,
when all the animals of the forest come creeping out.
The young lions roar for their prey, seeking their food from God.

Shields and Heals

Plants and animals have developed convoluted relations over millions of years, often involving the production and use of chemicals. Many plants generate chemicals as part of their natural defense mechanisms against herbivores and pathogens. Amusingly, some animals have learned to use these chemicals for their own benefit, using them for medicinal purposes, defense mechanisms, or even camouflage. Let us explore these enthralling connections and their ecological implication.

For many years we have noticed species like orangutans and chimpanzees using plants for their self-medication. They chose particular plants to treat sicknesses such as parasitic infections, gastrointestinal problems, and other skin issues. For example, chimpanzees in Tanzania's Gombe National Park have been seen chewing the bitter pith of Vernoniaamygdalina, which includes compounds with anti parasitic properties.

Some bird species integrate aromatic plants into their nests to keep away insects and parasites. The European starling and the blue tit are among others known to use plants like yarrow and wild carrot, which contain capricious compounds that prevent pests. There are several insect sequester toxins that they devour to use as a defense against predators. The monarch butterfly, for instance, feeds on milkweed plants during its larval stage to acquire toxic cardenolides, which make it unpalatable to birds and other predators. Similarly, the cinnabar moth caterpillar feeds on ragwort, storing alkaloids, which provide a chemical defense against predation. Some insects use plant chemicals to blend into their environment, effectively camouflaging themselves from predators. The peppered moth caterpillar can change its coloration to match the twigs it rests on, a process influenced by the intake of plant chemicals.

Plants, like the bullhorn acacia, produce nectar and house ants in their hollow thorns. In return, the ants protect the plant from herbivores by attacking any animals that attempts to feed on it. The plant's nectar contains chemicals that are attractive to the ants but not to other potential herbivores.

The use of plant chemicals by animals for medicinal purposes, defense mechanisms, and camouflage is a testament to the complex and dynamic relationships within ecosystems. These interactions draw attention to the importance of chemical ecology in understanding the natural world and underscore the interconnectedness of all living organisms.

Invisible Link

All things share the same breath—the beast, the tree, the man. The air shares its spirit with all the life it supports.

It is the invisible link between flora and fauna, but without it both cannot exist. Nature is an obscure web of interrelated relationships, with plants and animals relying heavily on each other for survival. Among these connections, one of the most fundamental and often ignored links is the exchange of oxygen and carbon dioxide. This invisible link is essential for the existence of both flora and fauna.

Oxygen and carbon dioxide are essential gases in the earth's atmosphere, facilitating the processes of respiration and photosynthesis. These two gasses are responsible for the existence of life and growth. Plants, algae, and particular bacteria use sunlight to convert carbon dioxide and water into glucose and oxygen. This process arises in the chloroplasts of plant cells, with chlorophyll incarcerating the light energy. Oxygen, a byproduct of photosynthesis, is released into the atmosphere, providing the essential gas for animal and human respiration

Animals, and humans, inhale oxygen and use it to break down glucose into carbon dioxide, water, and energy. This process occurs in the mitochondria of cells. Carbon dioxide, a byproduct of respiration, is exhaled by animals and taken up by plants to fuel photosynthesis. This exchange of gases forms a symbiotic relationship between plants and animals, each providing what the other needs to survive: Without this cycle, the balance of gases in the atmosphere would be disrupted, leading to dire consequences for all forms of life.

This invisible link ensures the stability of ecosystems: In conclusion, the invisible link of oxygen and carbon dioxide is fundamental to the coexistence of plants and animals. This exchange forms the backbone of life on earth and stresses the importance of conserving natural habitats and reducing activities that harm this delicate balance. Understanding and respecting this invisible link is crucial for maintaining the health and sustainability of our planet's ecosystems.

Conclusion

In this conclusion, I would like to mention the poem "Nature's Song" by Krystal Naomi Fernandes, a ten-year-old girl. She wrote this poem to pass the time during her spring break. It beautifully captures the essence of the spring season and vividly portrays various animals living in harmony.

> Nature's Song
> In the light of dawn's first ray,
> Rabbits and bunnies come out to play.
> Deer prance gently through the trees,
> While birds sing songs in the cool spring breeze.
> Mice rustle softly by the lake's side,
> Where flowers bloom and petals glide.

> Trees stand tall with leaves so bright,
> As the sun paints the sky with golden light.
> The river hums a peaceful tune,
> Underneath the blue sky, a silver moon.

A quiet, selfless dependence on one another is what makes the animal and plant kingdoms beautiful. Their communication transcends words; it's the language of being, each element playing its role in life's design. Nature, like a masterful weaver, intertwines flora and fauna with threads of sustenance, binding them in a cycle of mutual giving.

The book of Job 12:7–12 reminds us that true listening involves both our ears and our hearts.

> But ask the animals, and they will teach you; the birds of the air, and they will tell you; ask the plants of the earth, and they will teach you; and the fish of the sea will declare to you. Who among all these does not know that the hand of the Lord has done this? In his hand is the life of every living thing and the breath of every human being. Does not the ear test words as the palate tastes food? Is wisdom with the aged and understanding in length of days?

Every creature's breath and every being's pulse are in His hand. Wisdom isn't solely a characteristic of the elderly; it's found in the rustling leaves, birdsong at sunrise, and life's quiet perseverance. A divine author is evident in creation's harmony, watching over every relationship, every secret link, and every life-sustaining breath.

Nature's artistry reflects the Creator's wisdom and love, a silent symphony echoing His presence.

I would conclude this chapter by stating that I have deliberately excluded discussions on the interdependence between animals and other animals or plants and other plants. Instead, this chapter primarily focuses on the relationship between flora and fauna.

NERVES

Commotion all around,
Amid the mist of noise,
One voice stood out—
"It's not over."
I took a deep breath.

Brethren in coats all around,
Clad in white and green screens,
Yet I saw red—vivid, stark only on me.
One saw the graph go still,
But I felt—it was not.

Pushing, pulling, hands all around,
I felt their touch,
Yet the pain burned elsewhere.
A gloved hand pinched,
And I moved—just a finger.

I did not know what had happened.
Though I was an eyewitness,
Yet they said—
"Nerves are damaged."
"Unless they connect, he won't be whole."
I knew the truth,
But I could not speak, nor walk.
A silent battle between life and death
For I was the patient
In the doctor's hands.

Part II

Introduction

In this second part, we will explore the impact of human greed on flora and fauna. We must strive to embody the selflessness of the Native Indians, who recognized all of God's creatures not merely for their utility but as ends in themselves, offering praise to God simply by their existence.

Personifying the earth as a sister, much like St. Francis did, Pope Francis writes in the introduction of his encyclical *Laudato Si'* that humanity has committed many sins—against nature, against God, and against one another—by greedily consuming more than we need and wasting precious resources meant for the good of all.

In the opening chapter of the encyclical, he addresses these issues in detail. As he reminds us, "Human beings too are creatures of this world," and therefore, widespread environmental degradation does not only harm natural resources, it also harms human life.

Human beings were never granted unlimited authority to exploit the earth as they pleased. Accumulating excessive private property at the expense of others is not in accordance with God's will. The earth is a gift—meant for all and entrusted to the stewardship of all. This means its resources must be shared equitably and, at the same time, respected in their own right. Creation possesses an inherent dignity beyond its usefulness to humanity.

One of the greatest challenges we face is the adoption of a technocratic mindset—the belief that science and technology are the highest forms of truth, capable of solving any problem, and thereby justifying the reduction of the natural world to mere exploitable resources. In the following chapters, we will attempt to understand the suffering of plants and animals caused by human selfishness.

In the final chapter, we will explore flora and fauna as part of God's creation and our responsibility to protect them. We will also discuss how we can actively contribute to the preservation of the natural world. Pope Francis, in *Laudato Si'*, emphasizes the urgency of this mission: "The urgent challenge to protect our common home includes a concern to bring the whole human family together to seek a sustainable and integral development, for we know that things can change. The Creator does not abandon us; he never forsakes his loving plan or repents of having created us. Humanity still has the ability to work together in building our common home. Here I want to recognize, encourage, and thank all those striving in countless ways to guarantee the protection of the home, which we share. Particular appreciation is owed to those who tirelessly seek to resolve the tragic effects of environmental degradation on the lives of the world's poorest. Young people demand change. They wonder how anyone can claim to be building a better future without thinking of the environmental crisis and the sufferings of the excluded."

This powerful message reminds us that caring for creation is both a moral duty and a collective responsibility. By working together, we can protect the environment and build a sustainable future for generations to come.

Chapter 4

In the Name of Development

Let's start this chapter by examining a crucial part of William Wordsworth's 1807 sonnet "The World Is Too Much with Us." Wordsworth, a key figure in English Romanticism, laments humanity's estrangement from nature. He holds industrial society responsible for substituting that bond with materialism.

Composed during the First Industrial Revolution (mid-eighteenth to early nineteenth centuries), this poem is by Wordsworth, during a time of great technological and mechanical advances. British life underwent a profound transformation during this period, marked by rapid industrialization, urbanization, and a growing disconnect from nature. The poet grieves this shift, viewing it as a weakening of the spiritual and emotional connection between humanity and nature.

This chapter will analyze the poem's concluding lines.

> It moves us not. Great God! I'd rather be
> A Pagan suckled in a creed outworn;
> So might I, standing on this pleasant lea,
> Have glimpses that would make me less forlorn;
> Have sight of Proteus rising from the sea;
> Or hear old Triton blow his wreathèd horn.

Wordsworth begins this passage with the exclamation, "It moves us not." Here, he expresses frustration that people are no longer emotionally stirred by the beauty of nature. Instead, their focus is consumed by material concerns like wealth and industrial progress.

The poet then declares, "Great God! I'd rather be / A Pagan suckled in a creed outworn," meaning he would rather follow an ancient, nature-worshipping belief system than be part of a society that ignores the natural world. Although he thinks pagan traditions are outdated, he believes they acknowledged nature's spiritual importance.

By stating, "So might I, standing on this pleasant lea, / Have glimpses that would make me less forlorn," Wordsworth implies that nature, abandoned by modern society, would offer solace and purpose to a pagan.

In the lines, "Have sight of Proteus rising from the sea; / Or hear old Triton blow his wreathèd horn," the poet invokes Greek mythology to emphasize the lost connection between humans and nature. The sea gods Proteus and Triton, with their powers of transformation and wave control, embody a world where nature was revered as magical and godlike.

Wordsworth uses this text to critique the modern world's alienation from nature's spiritual harmony. He suggests that even the "outworn" Pagan beliefs, which revered the natural world, would be preferable to the soulless materialism of his time. He uses mythology to paint a picture of a world where nature remains magical and vital, a world different from our current monotonous, industrialized reality.

From this poem, we glean a deep sorrow at the destruction inflicted in the pursuit of progress. Wordsworth mourns the loss of flora and fauna and expresses a desire to return to a time before industrialization and colonization disrupted the natural balance.

This chapter details the historical exploitation and destruction of nature by humans in their quest for modern comforts. We should heed Wordsworth's warning, which is very relevant today, and rethink our priorities before we are entirely disconnected from nature.

The devastating environmental impact of human progress will also be explored, focusing on how countless plant and animal species have been endangered or driven to extinction in the name of development.

You Need to Know

"You need to know" was a deceptive mantra often used by colonizers to manipulate indigenous peoples. It was a call that ignored the voices and acumen of the native inhabitants, silencing their perspectives. Under this semblance of supposed knowledge sharing, colonizers imposed their way of life, exploiting the native flora and fauna for their own benefit. Though colonialism is not a modern trend, its stories are still told today. It's a political-economic phenomenon where numerous European nations discovered, conquered, and settled. In the sixteenth century, colonialism transformed unfalteringly because of technological advancement in navigation that began to connect more isolated parts of the world.

To better understand, let's examine Chief Seattle's speech: a powerful plea for ecological responsibility and indigenous rights. Chief Seattle's speech powerfully illustrates the callous disregard for Native American values shown by colonizers, contrasting their treatment of land and nature with indigenous perspectives. In 1854, Chief Seattle, a renowned leader of the Suquamish and Duwamish tribes, gave a memorable speech in Washington. His people recognized him as a prominent leader, wise and insightful.

Chief Seattle's speech balanced acceptance of white settlement with a plea for peaceful, respectful coexistence. Yet hidden beneath the surface of this diplomatic approach was a strong critique of Western civilization's exploitative habits. With great passion, he championed Native American land rights, stating land is not property but a sacred element essential for life.

Ecological responsibility was a key topic in his speech. In a warning about environmental exploitation, Chief Seattle highlighted the crucial link between nature (forests, rivers, animals, air) and humanity, predicting severe repercussions for its disregard. He famously declared, "Whatever befalls the earth befalls the sons of the earth," emphasizing that actions harming nature ultimately harm humankind. This prophetic warning is even more relevant now, given the world's struggles with climate change, deforestation, and dwindling natural resources.

Moreover, Chief Seattle questioned the Western view of land ownership, viewing nature not as a commodity. Alternatively, Native

American philosophy regarded land as a living organism, to be treasured and conserved for those to come. He urged people to be earth's caretakers, not exploiters, stressing a profound spiritual bond with nature. His words emphasized humanity's inseparable connection with nature.

Chief Seattle's speech continues to be a powerful plea for environmental awareness and respect for Native American cultures. His wisdom reminds us that sustainability and respect for nature aren't just ideals; they're essential for future generations' survival. Worldwide, his lasting message inspires environmentalists, policymakers, and rights supporters.

Polyculture Anoints Monoculture

Indigenous practices included sustainable monoculture, showing respect for the land and preserving biodiversity. Conversely, colonizers' introduction of widespread polyculture, while boosting yields, resulted in deforestation, soil degradation, and resource depletion. Colonial farming, unlike indigenous practices, which maintained ecological balance, prioritized profit over the environment, leading to long-term damage.

Colonization had significant, and frequently devastating, impact on flora and fauna across the world. As European powers expanded their empires, they brought about ecological transformation that altered ecosystems. They cleared huge plots of forests for agriculture, timber, and settlements. This led to the destruction of natural habitats, driving away animals and burning plant species to extinction. They introduced large-scale agricultural farms, often growing cash crops like sugar, tobacco, and cotton. This required extensive land clearing, which replaced diverse ecosystems with monocultures, reducing biodiversity. During the nineteenth and early twentieth centuries, people exploited the Amazon rainforest for its natural resources, including rubber, timber, and agricultural land. The Rubber Boom (late nineteenth century) led to the clearing of enormous areas of forest to establish rubber plantations. They cleared land for cattle ranching, which continues to be a major cause of deforestation in the Amazon. The destruction of the Amazon rainforest has had catastrophic effects on biodiversity, leading to the loss of countless species, some of which were never documented by science.

In the Caribbean, colonizers cleared forests on islands such as Hispaniola (modern-day Haiti and the Dominican Republic) and Jamaica to establish sugarcane plantations. Colonizers cleared vast tracts of land in the region to establish sugarcane plantations for export to Europe, making the sugar industry one of the primary drivers of deforestation. This deforestation led to soil erosion, loss of biodiversity, and the destruction of habitats for native species. The introduction of monoculture-cultivated area also made the land more vulnerable to pests and diseases, further destabilizing the ecosystem.

From Grinding to Mining

Colonizers with greed grind the ground for the mining of the natural recourses. The extraction of minerals such as gold, silver, and coal by colonizers caused severe ecological degradation. In places like South Africa and South America, mining operations led to soil erosion, water pollution, and the destruction of landscapes. The removal of topsoil and vegetation for mining also disrupted habitats, leading to the displacement of wildlife and the loss of biodiversity.

For instance, the state of Minas Gerais in Brazil was a major site for gold and iron mining during the colonial era and beyond. The mining activities led to the deforestation of sizeable areas, contributing to soil erosion and losing habitats. Another example would be the diamond mines in Kimberley, South Africa, some of the largest and most productive in the world. The excavation of massive open-pit mines, such as the Big Hole, caused severe landscape destruction. The mining activities disrupted local flora and fauna, and the intense demand for wood to support the mining infrastructure led to deforestation in the neighboring areas.

Invasive Species

European settlers brought with them livestock such as cattle, sheep, and pigs, and pets like dogs and cats. These animals often became invasive, in contrast with or preying on native species, leading to population declines or extinctions. As an example, the Polynesians introduced the feral pig

(Sus scrofa) to Hawaiian Island around fifteen years ago, and later in the eighteenth century, Europeans introduced another pig species (Brower, 1985). For the Hawaiian Island and its rainforest, feral pigs are an invasive species because they eat massive vegetation, causing native plant extinction and soil erosion. What makes feral pigs such an enormous menace for the Hawaiian rainforests are their peculiar hunt for food. The feral pigs alter the forest condition to the extent that the forest floor can no longer sustain any native plant species. This is done by aggressive uprooting tree and underground plant masses with their trunks, erosion of the forest soil with their massive consumption of understory plants, and creating an opportunity for invasive plants (Diong, 1982). Native plants like Ohi'a (Metrosideros polymorpha Gaud), and Koa (Acacia koa A. Gray) once dominated the forest floor, but now are now overrun by invasive species (Murakane, 2002). This behavior also led to the decline of several native plant species and contributed to the endangerment and extinction of native birds, like the Hawaiian crow ('Alalā), which suffered from habitat loss and predation by the pigs.

Overexploitation

The indigenous people hunted the animals but did not waste any part. Colonizers hunted the native fauna excessively for food, fur, and other purposes. They only used what they wanted and wasted the rest. Many species, such as the passenger pigeon in North America or the dodo in Mauritius, were driven to extinction because of unsustainable hunting practices.

The large-scale killing of buffalo (American bison) in Canada by colonizers had devastating effects on both the buffalo populations and the indigenous peoples who depended on them for the various needs. During the nineteenth century, European colonizers and huntsmen targeted buffalo for their hides, which were in high demand for leather goods. The mass slaughter was also driven by the desire to deteriorate indigenous populations by removing their primary food source and disrupting their way of life.

Buffalo hunting became industrialized, with hunters butchering thousands of animals in a single season. Hunters would kill the buffalo in wasteful ways, only taking their hides and sometimes their tongues, and leave the rest of the animal to rot. This indefensible hunting practice led to the near extinction of the buffalo, with the population plummeting from millions to just a few hundred by the late 1800s. The near extinction of the buffalo is one of the most tragic examples of the environmental and cultural destruction brought about by a colonial expansion in North America.

Another relevant example is of colonizers hunting elephants in Asia and Africa extensively for their ivory tusks, which were highly valued in Europe and beyond for crafting ornaments, piano keys, and various luxury items. This insatiable demand for ivory fueled widespread hunting, leading to the large-scale slaughter of elephants. As a result, elephant populations in many regions declined.

In the world of creatures with feathers, the dodo bird is one of the most famous examples of human-induced extinction. A large, flightless bird once native to the island of Mauritius in the Indian Ocean, the dodo was mightier than a turkey and weighed about twenty-three kilograms. The dodo had blue-gray feathers, an enormous head, and tiny, worthless wings. They likely nested on the ground and laid a single egg. Unfortunately, humans wiped out the species less than years after its discovery. Portuguese sailors discovered the birds around 1507. The birds had no natural predators, so they were unafraid of humans. These sailors, and others to come, quickly decimated the dodo population as an easy source of fresh meat for their voyages. As humans settled on the island, loss of habitat further threatened the birds. Humans also brought animals, such as pigs and monkeys, which ate the vulnerable eggs and competed with the dodos for food. Overharvesting of the birds, combined with habitat loss and a losing competition with the newly introduced animals, was too much for the dodos to survive.

These are the some of the negative impacts of colonization on flora and fauna in the name of discovery. These were often profound and long-lasting, so the legacy of colonization continues to affect biodiversity and environmental protection efforts today.

The Torch of Revolution

Let us explore the second subtopic of this chapter the industrial Revolution. There was a vast opposition to the Industrial Revolution by various authors and poets. Among the most outspoken critics of industrialization was William Blake, whose 1804 poem, "Jerusalem," vividly conveys his anxieties about its effects on England.

Blake juxtaposes England's former natural beauty against its grim, industrialized "satanic" present in Jerusalem. By questioning Jesus's presence on England's green hills, the poem expresses nostalgia for a time before factories and machines. Industrialization's severing of humanity's connection to the divine and its creation of social evils, such as child labor, poverty, and corruption, are criticized by Blake through biblical and mythological references.

Although he grieves, Jerusalem's story doesn't conclude in despair. Instead, it issues a call to action, a pledge to combat industrialization's destructive effects and revive England's lost beauty and harmony. With potent imagery and unyielding spirit, he depicts Jerusalem as a timeless symbol of resistance against oppression and a vision for a better, more just world.

Let us throw some light on the topic the torch of Revolution. The torch flashes and dispels darkness that illuminates what was once invisible. Similarly, the Enlightenment period shed light on the path to the Industrial Revolution, enlightening humans with innovative ideas and an array of possibilities.

Enlightenment, which dominated Europe during the seventeenth and eighteenth centuries, often receives distinction for advancing science, reason, and human rights. However, this period also had some negative consequences for animals and plants. While the primary focus of the Enlightenment was on human progress, these advancements sometimes came at the expense of the natural world. This anthropocentric worldview emphasized human reason and the capacity to control and manipulate nature. Its views led to the negative conception that humans had the right to exploit natural resources, including flora and fauna, for their advantage.

The Industrial Revolution, which began in the late eighteenth century, brought about massive technological, economic, and social changes.

While it led to significant advancements in human societies, it also had devastating effects on the natural environment, particularly on plants and animals. Here's how the Industrial Revolution contributed to the destruction of wildlife and ecosystems.

Urge for Urbanization

The speedy expansion of cities during the Industrial Revolution required extensive land clearing for accommodation, factories, and infrastructure. This caused the annihilation of natural habitats, displacing innumerable species of plants and animals. London is the apt example which experienced rapid urban intensification, becoming one of the major cities in the world. The demand for housing, industrial units, and road and rail networks led to the extensive clearing of forests and farmlands surrounding the city.

The European beaver, the wild boar, and other species that relied on these ancient woodlands and wetlands around London had to leave because of human activities, and some people hunted them to extinction in the region. Losing greenery also affected bird populations, with species such as the red kite and peregrine falcon number dwindling because of habitat loss and pollution.

New York City's birth serves as another example. The transformation of the natural water systems on the island into land or burial resulted in the loss of the wetlands that had supported diverse ecosystems. The city's expansion into the surrounding areas also destroyed habitats in regions like Long Island, leading to the decline of species such as the heath hen, which became extinct in the early twentieth century.

Turing Woods into Wood

In the name of revolution, vast forests were transformed into mere logs of wood. Whole woodlands were cleared on a massive scale to supply lumber for construction, firewood for factories, and land for agriculture. For instance, in the eighteenth and nineteenth centuries, the European Alps endured extensive deforestation to supply timber for edifice and fuel for the growing industrial economy. This deforestation was compounded by agricultural expansion. The clearing of forests in the Alps led to the decline of species that depended on the dense forest cover. For example, the Alpine ibex, which once roamed the lower forests, was driven to near extinction but has been partially restored through conservation efforts.

In British Columbia, Canada, the Great Bear Rainforest has been the victim of logging activities since the late nineteenth century. Regardless of ongoing preservation efforts, logging and industrial activities have persistently threatened this temperate rainforest. The loss of old-growth forest has impacted species, such as the Spirit bear (a rare white version of the black bear) and various salmon species that rely on healthy forest ecosystems for spawn grounds. The deforestation has led to habitat fragmentation and a decline in ecological integrity.

Pop of Pollution

The burning of coal and other fossil fuels in industrial units and steam engines released huge amount of pollutants into the environment. This caused air pollution, which harmed plants through acid rain and smog. It also impacted animals by contaminating their habitats. Industrial waste, including chemicals and heavy metals, were often discarded straight into bodies of water. This polluted water sources, leading to the death of marine life and the ruin of freshwater ecosystems. Industrial activities released toxic substances even into the soil, making it less productive and detrimental to plants. Contaminated soil also affected animals that relied on the land for food and habitat.

Irrational Hunt

The Industrial Revolution increased the demand for animal products, and as a consequence there was overhunting and overfishing. The persistent pursuit of resources like fur, ivory, and whale oil led to the extinction of many species. For instance, the fur trade, particularly for beaver pelts, was a major industry during the Industrial Revolution. People highly valued beaver fur for making hats and other clothing.

As a result, overhunting of beavers led to their near extinction in many parts of North America. The reduction of beaver populations also disrupted ecology, as beavers play a crucial role in creating wetlands and maintaining water systems.

In the water world, the demand for whale oil, which was used for lamps, lubrication, and later in the production of margarine and soap, drove intensive whaling in the eighteenth and nineteenth centuries. Humans hunted species like the blue whale, humpback whale, and right whale to the brink of extinction. The relentless pursuit of these marine mammals led to a dramatic decline in their populations, with some species still struggling to recover today.

Land Fragmentation

This title makes me think of Robert Frost's "Mending Wall" and its exploration of boundaries, nature, and human connection. In the lines, "There where it is we do not need the wall: / He is all pine and I am apple orchard. / My apple trees will never get across/ And eat the cones under his pines, I tell him," The speaker jokingly points out that nature doesn't need fences—apple trees won't encroach on pines. However, the neighbor stubbornly quotes the adage, "Good fences make good neighbors," highlighting their rigid adherence to tradition.

Feeling playful in the spring air, the speaker challenges this belief: "Spring is the mischief in me, and I wonder/ If I could put a notion in his head:/'Why do they make good neighbors? Isn't it / Where there are cows? But here there are no cows."

He contends that fences are only useful for containing livestock, a need absent in this situation. The poem shows how nature works together effortlessly, unlike humans, who create unnecessary divisions, making us wonder if walls create harmony or just isolation.

Animals and plants do not build walls; they coexist naturally, adapting to their surroundings without imposing barriers. Yet, humans cause divisions, establishing territories and dividing land with tangible and intangible boundaries.

For instance, the construction of roads, railways, and industrial infrastructure fragmented habitats, isolating animal populations and reducing genetic diversity. This fragmentation made it difficult for species to migrate, find food, and reproduce, leading to population declines. The construction of highways, particularly Interstate 75 (Alligator Alley) and other roads across southern Florida, has fragmented the habitat of the Florida panther, a critically endangered species.

Habitat fragmentation has isolated Florida panther populations, leading to inbreeding and a lack of genetic diversity, which increases the risk of genetic disorders and reduces overall fitness. The barriers created by roads also limit the panthers' ability to find new territories and mates, contributing to population decline. Wildlife underpasses and road-crossing structures have been implemented to mitigate these effects.

Human Meddling

The Industrial Revolution led to the growth and extensive use of chemical fertilizers and pesticides. These chemicals not only destroyed target pests but also had unintended effects on non-target species, including helpful insects, birds, and other wildlife. All this happens because of human interference in order increase quality and quantity of food grain.

DDT (dichlorodiphenyltrichloroethane) was a commonly used pesticide after its introduction in the 1940s. It was effective in repealing mosquito populations and agricultural pests, but it also has overwhelming effects on bird populations, particularly birds of prey like bald eagles, peregrine falcons, and ospreys. DDT mounts up in the food chain, leading to the thinning of eggshells in birds of prey. This results in prevalent reproductive failure and remarkable population declines. The bald eagle, for instance, became rare in the United States. The prohibition on DDT in the 1970s led to a slow recovery of these species, highlighting the unintended consequences of chemical pesticide use.

Neonicotinoids are a class of insecticides that became popular in the 1990s. Neonicotinoids serve the purpose of protecting crops from pests, but researchers have connected them to the decline of pollinators, specifically honeybees and other wild bees. Neonicotinoids affect the nervous systems of insects, leading to disorientation, reduced foraging ability, and death in bees. The decline in bee populations has significant ecological and economic consequences, as bees are crucial pollinators for many crops and wild plants. This has led to calls for restrictions on neonicotinoid used to protect pollinator health. Then each of these examples, the use of chemicals in agriculture, had unintended and often severe consequences for non target species and ecosystems. These effects underscore the need for careful consideration and regulation of chemicals used to protect biodiversity and environmental health.

Shift in Attitudes

The Industrial Revolution fostered a view of nature as a resource to be exploited for monetary gain rather than a coordination to be preserved. This shift in attitudes contributed to the widespread environmental degradation that accompanied industrial progress. The Industrial Revolution manifested a significant shift in human attitudes toward nature as society increasingly considered the natural world as a resource to be exploited for economic gain rather than as a system to be preserved. This shift in mindset had profound implications for environmental degradation.

Agricultural Escalation

The Agricultural Revolution, which coincided with the Industrial Revolution, saw the intensification of farming methods to hold up mounting urban populations. Innovations like the enclosure movement in England, which merged small farms into large, privately owned estates, increased agricultural efficiency but also led to the annihilation of traditional landscapes. They increasingly treated agricultural land as a commodity to exploit for yield, which led to the pervasive adoption of monoculture farming, deforestation, and filling of the wetlands. Many prioritized short-term gains over long-term environmental health, leading them to abandon traditional and more sustainable farming practices.

Industrial Optimism

The Industrial Revolution was characterized by a belief in the power of human ingenuity and technology to conquer nature. This attitude showed in projects like the construction of gigantic dams, the emptying of swamps for agricultural use, and the canalization of rivers for transportation. This technological optimism led people to believe that they could control and manipulate nature to fulfill human needs, often without considering the potential consequences. That nature existed to be "enhanced" or "controlled" for human benefit became prevalent, leading to large-scale environmental alterations that often resulted in habitat destruction and loss of biodiversity.

Byproduct of Progress

The first industrial cities, with their smoke-belching plants and polluted rivers, illustrated how environmental degradation was often perceived as an obvious consequence of evolution. In cities like London, people accepted industrial smog and river pollution as signs of economic success, even though they caused significant harm to public health and the environment. That environmental degradation was an adequate trade-off for economic growth became ingrained during the Industrial Revolution. The pursuit of industrial and economic expansion often led to the sacrifice of the health of ecosystems as people primarily viewed natural resources in terms of their economic value.

Anthropocentric Worldview

The Enlightenment stressed human rationality and our power to control and manipulate the natural world. This anthropocentric perspective fostered the belief that humans had the right to exploit natural resources, including animals and plants, for their benefit. The idea of using science and technology to control nature was championed by thinkers such as Francis Bacon. Although this method yielded substantial progress, it also spurred excessive natural resource consumption, frequently disregarding long-term environmental impacts.

In contrast, Henry David Thoreau's *Walden*, a collection of eighteen essays first published in 1854, offers a different perspective on humanity's relationship with nature. This book recounts a two-year experiment in simple living near Concord, Massachusetts, where Thoreau explored self-sufficiency and mindfulness. He constructed a modest cabin on Ralph Waldo Emerson's property, cultivated his sustenance, and devoted himself to nature, embracing a life of intention and profound contemplation on life's fundamentals.

Themes of labor, leisure, self-reliance, and individualism are explored in *Walden*, a cornerstone of New England Transcendentalism. The opening essay, "Economy," details the construction and cost of Thoreau's cabin, emphasizing the virtues of simplicity. In "Reading" and "Sounds," he reflects on literature and the importance of mindful living, while "Solitude" celebrates the companionship of nature over the distractions of society. Later essays, including "Higher Laws" and "Spring," explore morality, renewal, and humanity's profound relationship with nature.

Overlooked at first, *Walden* achieved significant twentieth-century recognition for its elegant prose and philosophical insights. Its meditations on life and nature ensure its status as a literary classic today. Readers continue to find inspiration in the book's profound insights and memorable passages, such as the famous lines, "The mass of men lead lives of quiet desperation," and, "If a man does not keep pace with his companions, perhaps it is because he hears a different drummer."

Scientific Experimentation

The Enlightenment saw a surge in scientific exploration, where European naturalists traveled all over the globe to collect plant and animal specimens. While this expanded scientific knowledge, it also led to the removal of species from their natural habitats, sometimes causing local extinctions. The practice of collecting specimens for study and display in museums often involved killing animals and harvesting plants. This sometimes led to the depletion of local populations and the disruption of ecosystems.

Ethical Attitudes

Although the Enlightenment advanced human rights and individual freedoms, these ideas did not extend to animals. The period's focus on rationality and human superiority often led to the justification of exploiting animals as resources, with little regard for their well-being. The pursuit of scientific knowledge during the Enlightenment sometimes involved practices like vivisection (dissection of live animals) for the sake of medical and biological investigation. This caused suffering to animals and reflected a broader disregard for their welfare. The objectification of nature was also prevalent during the Enlightenment period and emphasized on categorizing and classifying the natural world, as seen in the work of Carl Linnaeus. This led to a more detached view of nature. Individuals viewed plants and animals as objects to be studied and subjugated rather than recognizing them as living beings of intrinsic value.

Philosophical Interpretation

Enlightenment philosophers, including René Descartes, emphasized rationalism and often regarded animals as machines or automata without feelings. This view justified their use in experiments and as resources without ethical considerations. Some Enlightenment thinkers, like Jeremy Bentham, considered the suffering of animals, but the dominant utilitarian perspective still often justified the exploitation of animals and plants if it benefited the greater good of society.

    Above were some of the negative impacts of the Industrial Revolution on flora and fauna. However, we cannot deny the numerous advantages it brought to human civilization. The key question here is whether human beings pursued progress selfishly, focusing solely on their own benefits, or whether they also considered the needs of other living beings. To conclude, one cannot inherently say the enlightenment era is evil. To be more precise, humanity's greed has caused its more negative outcomes. Industrialization, while advancing progress and innovation, also led to the relentless exploitation of nature. Mary Oliver's poem "Of the Empire" powerfully conveys this theme.

In "Of the Empire," Oliver criticizes humanity's greed, industrial expansion, and environmental destruction. The untouched beauty of nature is contrasted with the devastation of civilization, showcasing the real cost of advancement. Humanity's inexorable pursuit of power and riches, and the resulting environmental damage, is the poem's lament for lost, pristine landscapes. With a reflective and poignant tone, Oliver questions the real value of such advancements and urges readers to reconsider their relationship with nature before it is irreversibly damaged.

Both the Industrial Revolution and Oliver's critique in "Of the Empire" remind us that progress, when driven by unchecked greed, can come at a significant cost. Yet, wise and responsible industrialization can harmonize with environmental protection, preventing innovation from harming nature.

The Modern Era

Here we on the third subsection of this chapter. Spanning from the nineteenth century to the present day, there has been unprecedented exploitation of animals and plants due to rapid industrialization, technological advancements, and population growth. While this period has brought about significant progress in many areas, it has also led to severe environmental degradation and the exploitation of natural resources, often at the expense of wildlife and ecosystems. Here's how the modern era has exploited animal and plant life:

Industrial fishing techniques, including trawling and long lining, have caused the overexploitation of fish populations and the destruction of marine habitats. Many fish species have been driven to the brink of collapse, and by catch (the capture of non-target species) has further threatened marine life. The burning of fossil fuels for energy and transportation, along with deforestation, has led to a significant increase in harmful gases, contributing to global climate change. Rising temperatures, changing precipitation patterns, and more frequent extreme weather events are altering habitats and threatening the survival of countless species. Increased carbon dioxide levels in the atmosphere are also causing ocean acidification, which affects marine life, particularly coral reefs and shellfish, by disrupting their ability to form shells and skeletons.

Farms in Clutches

The rise of industrial-scale animal farming, or factory farming, has led to the mass production of animals for food. These practices often involve inhumane conditions, such as overcrowding, confinement, and the use of antibiotics and growth hormones. The environmental impacts include water pollution, deforestation for grazing land, and harmful emissions from methane produced by livestock. Factory farming also contributes to the loss of wild habitats, as large areas of land are cleared to grow feed crops like soy and corn. The runoff from these farms pollutes waterways, harming aquatic life and contributing to dead zones in oceans.

Genetic Modification

Advances in genetic science have led to the development of genetically modified organisms (GMOs). While these can increase agricultural productivity, they can also reduce genetic diversity and potentially harm non-target species, including beneficial insects and soil microorganisms. This era of modernity has also seen the rise of biotechnology involving cloning and genetic engineering. While these technologies have potential benefits, they raise moral dilemmas and could lead to unintended consequences on living things.

Consumerism and Waste

The modern era is characterized by significant amounts of consumerism, leading to the overconsumption of natural resources. This has caused in the clearance of forests, mines, and the depletion of freshwater resources, all of which harm plants and animals. The production and disposal of waste, including toxic chemicals, electronic byproducts, and plastic, have further polluted the environment. This waste harms wildlife, pollutes ecology, and contributes to the degradation of natural habitats. Let's take an example: Agbogbloshie, a suburb of Accra, Ghana, is one of the world's largest electronic-waste dumpsites. E-waste from around the globe is transported here, where it is sorted out by informal workers, often without proper safety equipment. Toxic chemicals like lead, mercury, and cadmium from discarded electronics contaminate the soil, water, and air, posing severe health risks to the workers and surrounding communities. The combustion of electronic components to extract valuable metals also releases harmful toxins into the atmosphere.

Guinea Pig

Guinea pig a phrase used for a person on whom new ideas or techniques are tested. It has an origin from the experimentation done on animals before it is used on humans. The modern era has seen extensive use of animals in scientific research, cosmetics testing, and entertainment, often under conditions that cause suffering and distress to the animals involved. Here are some examples of animal testing and exploitation in the modern era: For many years, the cosmetics industry relied heavily on animal testing to ensure the safety of products like makeup, shampoos, and skin creams. Rabbits, guinea pigs, mice, and other animals were commonly used in tests, such as the Draize eye irritation test, where substances were applied directly to the eyes, often causing pain, blindness, or death. Although some countries have banned or limited animal testing for beauty products, it remains a practice in certain regions, leading to continued suffering for countless animals.

Primates, such as monkeys and chimpanzees, have been used extensively in biomedical research due to their genetic similarity to humans. Invasive procedures, including surgeries, drug testing, and neurological experiments, are often conducted on these animals. For example, in studies related to neuroscience, primates are sometimes exposed to brain implants, forced isolation, or food deprivation. These practices can cause significant psychological distress, physical pain, and even death. The use of primates in research has been a major ethical concern, leading to growing calls for alternative methods.

Entertainment

For decades, animals have been used in circuses and other forms of entertainment, often under harsh and inhumane conditions. Elephants, lions, and other wild animals are trained using force and fear to execute unnatural tricks for spectators. The animals are normally kept in small enclosures, subjected to long periods of confinement, and transported across long distances in cramped conditions. The physical and psychological stress of this exploitation often leads to health problems, behavioral issues, and shortened life spans. Public outcry and changing attitudes have led some countries and regions to ban the use of wild animals in circuses.

The modern era has brought about profound changes in the way humans interact with the natural world, often prioritizing economic growth and technological progress over environmental conservation. The exploitation of animals and plants during this period has led to significant ecological damage, loss of biodiversity, and ruined the ecosystems. These impacts continue to pose challenges for global conservation efforts as we grapple with the long-term consequences of economic progress and industrialization.

The Era of Digital Innovation

The last topic for reflection in this chapter is the Digital Revolution. The Digital Revolution has undoubtedly transformed the globe, but its environmental costs are significant. The demand for resources, energy, and infrastructure to support technological advancements has led to the exploitation of plants and animals, contributing to habitat destruction, pollution, and global warming. As we continue to advance technologically, it is crucial to balance innovation with sustainability, ensuring that the exploitation of natural resources does not prioritize over the planet's rich variety of species and ecological health.

The period of significant agricultural transformation, which began in the mid-twentieth century, was a result of the Green Revolution. It involved the widespread adoption of high-yielding crop varieties, chemical fertilizers, pesticides, and efficient irrigation techniques aimed at increasing food production to feed the growing global population. While the Green Revolution successfully boosted food production and eased hunger in numerous regions, it also had several adverse effects on wildlife, plants, and the environment as a whole. Here's how the Green Revolution adversely impacted the natural world:

The Green Revolution promoted the cultivation of some high-yielding crop varieties, often leading to monoculture farming. This practice abridged agricultural biodiversity, as traditional, diverse crops were replaced by a few dominant species. The loss of genetic diversity made crops more vulnerable to pests, diseases, and shifting environmental conditions.

Decline of Native Species

The emphasis on specific crops with high productivity led to the neglect and decline of native plant species, some of which were better adapted to local conditions and required fewer inputs, like water and fertilizers. The reduction in plant diversity also affected the animals that depended on these native plants for food and habitat.

Nutrient Depletion

The farming techniques promoted by the Green Revolution, including the repeated planting of the same crops, led to the depletion of soil nutrients. This necessitated the use of synthetic fertilizers, which further disrupted the natural nutrient cycles in the soil. The conversion of diverse ecosystems into large-scale monoculture farms, combined with the use of heavy machinery, resulted in heightened soil erosion. This not only reduced soil fertility but also contributed to the disappearance of living spaces for plants and animals that rely on healthy soil ecosystems.

Scarcity of Water Resources

The Green Revolution's emphasis on high-yielding crops often required large amounts of water for irrigation. This led to the over extraction of groundwater and the depletion of rivers and lakes, reducing the availability of water for natural ecosystems and the species that depend on them.

Resistance and Pest Outbreaks

Pesticide Resistance: The overuse of chemical pesticides led to resistance among many pest species. This resulted in the need for even more potent chemicals or larger quantities of pesticides, exacerbating the environmental and ecological impacts.

Secondary Pest Outbreaks: The elimination of natural predators through pesticide use sometimes led to secondary pest outbreaks, where previously controlled pest species became problematic, further disrupting ecosystems and agricultural systems.

Traditional Farming Practices

The Green Revolution often displaced traditional farming practices that were more sustainable and in harmony with local ecosystems. This shift led to the loss of traditional knowledge and practices that supported biodiversity and ecosystem health. The focus on crop production sometimes came at the expense of traditional livestock farming, leading to changes in grazing patterns and land use, which affected both domestic animals and wildlife.

Threat to Food Security

The emphasis on a restricted variety of high-productivity crops increased food production but also made the global food supply more vulnerable to pests, diseases, and changing environmental conditions. The loss of crop diversity threatens food security and the resilience of agricultural systems.

The Green Revolution brought about a significant increase in food production, which was necessary to feed a growing global population. However, it also had unintended negative consequences for animals, plants, and the environment. The intensive agricultural practices promoted during this period led to biodiversity loss, habitat destruction, pollution, and other environmental issues that continue to affect ecosystems today. As the world faces new challenges in agriculture and food security, there is a growing recognition of the need for more sustainable practices to protect the environment while ensuring adequate food production.

Conclusion

"Earth provides enough to satisfy every man's need, but not every man's greed," said Mohandas K. Gandhi.

By and large, development is essential for the betterment of the human race, and we should not stand in opposition to it. Yet, we must strive for progress responsibly and with balance. Let me use the allegory of nail cutting to illustrate this concept.

Fingernails grow continuously, and while some people trim them annually, others do so monthly. Regardless of frequency, we only remove the excess growth, being careful not to cut too deeply and cause pain. Likewise, nature—its flora and fauna—is available for our use, but it must be treated with the same mindful restraint.

If we indiscriminately cut down trees without replanting, we disrupt the delicate equilibrium of our environment. Similarly, excessive slaughter of animals upsets the ecological balance. Harvesting what is surplus is justifiable, but overexploitation leads to harm—just as cutting nails too short causes pain.

True progress is defined by thoughtful stewardship, not rampant consumption. Sustainable growth is not about rejecting development but about ensuring that consumption is balanced with restoration. If we fail to protect our environment, we risk halting progress entirely.

As Dalai Lama wisely reminds us: "Peace and the survival of life on Earth as we know it are threatened by human activities that lack a commitment to humanitarian values. The destruction of nature and its resources results from ignorance, greed, and a lack of respect for Earth's living things." By embracing wisdom and restraint, we can secure a future where progress and nature coexist in harmony.

GARDENER

Took off the petals, leaving it bare,
Neither for his gain nor for others to share,
Yet the garden was gentle, forgiving his strife
For he was but a child, still learning of life.

She cut the stem and stole the bloom
To adorn her home, dispelling its gloom.
It pleased her guests, though nature paid already,
Yet the garden stayed silent for she was the lady.

He touched none but pruned with care,
Not for his gain but for the plant laid bare.
His hands gave life, spreading the manure,
Yet the garden bloomed, though the gardener was but newer.

Nature is the garden, vast and deep,
And we, its keepers, sow what we reap.
Are we like the child, who takes with greed?
Or the woman, who claims, yet neglects the need?
Or shall we be like the gardener, humble and wise,
Who nurtures the garden, where true beauty lies?
Let us know nature well, to keep it whole,
For giving, not taking, should be our soul.

Chapter 5

Independent Prison

To the plants and animals, the blue ocean, vast sky, and green land may appear as spaces of freedom, but to me, it's an independent prison. In truth, they are not. They are held captive by the relentless grip of pollution. Human beings created this prison. They are innocent, yet they suffer from the selfishness of others.

Pollution, a menace created by humans, demonstrates a lack of consideration for other life forms. Our ability to control it doesn't stop us from taking more than required from nature, driven by human comfort and selfishness. This overconsumption transforms need into want, leading to waste and destruction. Need is what sustains us, while want is what we take for our comforts—often at the cost of other living creatures.

We fail to understand the pain we cause by our negligence. Albert Einstein put it this way: "Your fervent wishes can only find fulfillment if you succeed in attaining love and understanding of men, and animals, and plants, and stars, so that every joy becomes your joy and every pain your pain."

Let's consider Rachel Carson's insightful words: "The most alarming of all man's assaults upon the environment is the contamination of air, earth, rivers, and sea with dangerous and even lethal materials. This pollution is for the most part irrecoverable; the chain of evil it initiates not only in the world that must support life but in living tissues is for the most part irreversible. In this now universal contamination of the environment, chemicals are the sinister and little-recognized partners of radiation in changing the very nature of the world—the very nature of its life."

Silent Spring (1962) by Carson vividly portrays the destructive impact of uncontrolled industrial growth and human avarice. The quote above can be found in the same book. Americans were astonished by her disclosures on the hazards of the overuse of pesticides. Starting her story, she painted a picture of a fictional but frightening town lacking birdsong, bees, and healthy children, subtly suggesting a future where nature is silenced.

Carson's in-depth research showed how pesticides, like DDT, contaminated water, soil, and living organisms, harming insects, birds, fish, and people. She challenged the chemical industry and regulators and debunked the idea of a nature-humanity divide by masterfully combining scientific research with compelling narratives. Her point was simple: Humanity's destruction of nature threatens our existence.

The impact of her work was monumental. *Silent Spring* ignited a wave of environmental activism that resulted in the formation of the US Environmental Protection Agency in 1970 and the subsequent banning of DDT in 1972. However, despite these wins, the use of other harmful chemicals, such as glyphosate in Roundup, remains a serious health concern and potentially linked to cancer.

Carson's warnings remain as relevant today as they were in the 1960s. Their actions have driven movements advocating for organic agriculture, stricter pesticide controls, and legal action against chemical firms. Similar to Mary Oliver's "Of the Empire," which criticizes industrialization and unchecked greed, *Silent Spring* reminds us that genuine progress requires profound environmental responsibility. Future generations are inspired by her lasting legacy to protect both human and environmental health.

Invisibles' Visible Effect

Despite air being invisible, we can definitely sense its existence. Invisible pollutants and gases have visible effects on both flora and fauna when they mix with the air. The presence of this pollution not only shortens the lifespan of many living beings but also contributes to various infections and illnesses.

Grant me the permission to share a comical anecdote about the "Gas Chamber."

He earned the title for good reason. The tranquility of a study hall was shattered when a loud fart unexpectedly erupted, resulting in uncontrollable laughter. Without thinking, everyone pinched their noses, and he earned the nickname the "Gas Chamber," despite the fart not being odoriferous.

From then on, in the minor seminary, anytime there was a faint whiff of something unpleasant, whether in the study hall or the refectory, all eyes would turn to him. He was a good-natured soul, always taking it with a pinch of salt and laughing at himself. In his honor, many others discreetly released their own "silent contributions."

Although the air and the fart are invisible in this example, the reaction of pinching the nose is evident and vivid. When harmful gases pollute the invisible air, it becomes evident through negative effects on living organisms.

Battling Leaves

As we know plant leaves can be damaged by the presence of sulfur dioxide (SO_2) and nitrogen oxides (NO_x) in the air. These unseen gases dissolving in water vapor result in the formation of acids that have negative effects on plant surfaces and stomata, preventing both gas exchange and photosynthesis.

The amalgamation of rainwater with pollutants, such as sulfur dioxide and nitrogen oxides, creates acid rain, which affects soil chemistry. This can leach essential nutrients from the soil, like calcium and magnesium, making it harder for plants to absorb the nutrients they need. Ground-level ozone, a major component of smog, directly affects plants by damaging cells in leaves, which reduces their ability to photosynthesize, grow, and reproduce. The presence of pollutants can hinder plant growth and reproduction, causing a decrease in crop yield and forest degradation. Pollution-exposed plants are usually more vulnerable to diseases, pests, and extreme weather.

Chemical Torture

High levels of particulate matter (PM), ozone, and other harmful chemicals in the air can cause lung damage, reduce lung function, and lead to respiratory diseases in animals. While plants are damaged by air pollution, it can also lead to a disorder in the food chain. The food supply for herbivores may decrease, causing health issues for animals higher in the food chain due to the accumulation of toxins in the plants they consume. Acid rain and other forms of air pollution can degrade ecosystems like forests, rivers, and lakes, making it difficult for animals to find suitable habitats. Overall, air pollution creates a cascade of negative effects on both plants and animals, disrupting ecosystems and biodiversity.

We, as human beings, can take preventive measures to reduce air pollution. For example, during the COVID-19 pandemic, despite the virus being invisible, people started wearing masks and maintaining social distance to protect themselves. Similarly, proactive steps can be taken to minimize air pollution and its harmful effects. However, unlike humans, animals are innocent and vulnerable; they cannot protect themselves and often fall victim to the dangers of air pollution. It is our responsibility to ensure a cleaner environment for all living beings.

Stream to River

As the stream flows from the spring through the mountains, it remains as pure as a virgin. Though it rushes down with strength, carving its path toward the river, it nurtures the living organisms within. It dodges pebbles, spares the fish, and flows untouched by human contamination.

However, when it kisses the river, gradual adulteration seeps in. By the time the river reaches the sea, it tests the lick of oil and indigestible plastic.

In the mountains, the water is a life-giving force, nourishing nature in its pristine form. Yet, when it falls into human hands, its value is neglected, and as a consequence, marine life suffers.

Inevitable Bait

Bait lures the fish to its doom, but inevitable bait is more subtle—it affects the fish even when it's not aware of the trap. Let me illustrate with example.

A man watched a grand house from a distance. The lady of the house was known for her love of gold jewelry. Early each morning, her husband left for work to avoid the rush, and soon after, the school bus would honk to collect the children. One such morning, while the lady was busy tidying up and preparing lunch, the doorbell rang. Distracted, she removed her oven mitts and hurried to the door. Peeking through the peephole, she saw a well-dressed salesman holding irresistible trinkets. Her hands moved almost instinctively to open the door.

Once inside, the salesman's charm and words were as compelling as his products. But then, his demeanor shifted—he became aggressive, demanding gold and money. She screamed, but before anyone could respond, he silenced her forever and left with the gold she wore.

In a different story, a similar kind of inevitable bait appeared in our own lives. My family's properties are abundant with cashew trees, and in May, the nuts are harvested and sold like gold. Many moons ago, I suppose before my birth, a woman came to our door, claiming to want to buy cashew nuts. My mother, eager to make a sale, called my grandmother. They began bargaining with the woman, but her words had an enchanting quality. Slowly, she hypnotized them with her charm. By the end of the conversation, my mother and grandmother unknowingly gave away all of the cashew nuts without receiving a single coin.

In the first case, it was the bait itself—the salesman's intent was to destroy, much like a fisherman whose goal is to catch and kill. The woman, unaware of his true motives, became the victim. Similarly, the fisherman doesn't care about the fish's desires; he uses bait to lure it to its doom.

In the second case, it's a clear example of inevitable bait. My family members were helpless, unaware of what was happening. They fell victim to the woman's manipulation. Though the destruction wasn't as severe as the first case, the impact was significant. No sale meant no income, leading to financial strain for the entire family. Just as contaminated water may not seem dangerous to the fish at first, it slowly affects them without their knowledge, leading to harm over time.

In these two stories, the house represents the water bodies, and the individuals visiting symbolize human beings. The households represent the fish. Some visitors, like the salesman, come to kill, while others, like the woman, destroy the resources that provide sustenance. Human selfishness put the life of animal and plant species at risk.

Swimming Flora

Pollutants, such as excess nitrogen and phosphorus from agricultural runoff, cause nutrient imbalances in water bodies. This leads to *eutrophication*, a process where excessive nutrient loads cause rapid algae growth (algal blooms). Algal blooms block sunlight, disrupting photosynthesis for aquatic plants and leading to oxygen depletion. Low oxygen levels make it difficult for fish and other aquatic organisms to survive, often resulting in mass die-offs.

Pollutants like heavy metals (e.g., lead, mercury) and industrial chemicals in water can be toxic to plants, inhibiting their growth or causing death. Toxic substances can accumulate in plant tissues, affecting their metabolism and reducing their reproductive success. These toxins accumulate in the tissues of animals through a process called *bioaccumulation* and become more concentrated higher up the food chain, affecting predators (e.g., birds, fish, mammals).

Acidic or alkaline water, often due to industrial waste, mining runoff, or acid rain, can damage aquatic plants. Changes in pH can also affect nutrient availability in soil and water, which negatively impacts plant growth. Certain pollutants, such as pharmaceuticals and pesticides, can interfere with the endocrine systems of animals. This can lead to reproductive issues, abnormal development, and population declines in species like fish and amphibians.

Water pollution can destroy habitats essential for plant life. Oil spills, for instance, create physical barriers for plants by coating surfaces, which blocks sunlight and reduces oxygen exchange in the water. Oil spills, plastic waste, and chemical pollutants can destroy or degrade aquatic habitats, such as coral reefs, wetlands, and rivers, which many species depend on for shelter, feeding, and breeding. Marine animals, like sea turtles, dolphins, and seabirds, are particularly vulnerable to habitat loss.

In coastal areas, pollution can increase the salinity of freshwater bodies, damaging freshwater plants that cannot tolerate high salt concentrations. For instance, plastic pollution is often mistaken for food by marine animals, leading to ingestion and entanglement, which can be fatal.

Water pollution poses severe risks to both plant and animal life, disrupting natural processes and threatening the health of entire ecosystems.

Alien in the Stomach

An alien in the stomach will always create turmoil; much like pollution in the land disrupts nature's balance. While the human stomach has the metabolism to digest various types of food, there are some seeds it simply can't process. Let me tell you about how my friend viewed food.

Rain or shine, we would trek three kilometers to school, unless we took the shortcut. It wasn't a smooth, tarred road but one surrounded with tress of wild fruits. During the off-season, tender coconuts were our saviors and quenched our parched throats. We spent our days outdoors, and our parents would pinch our ears to drag us back inside. The rush to school was always quick, but coming back was a lazy loiter.

On our way home, we sometimes stole fruits, and other times, we indulged in the bounty of orphaned fruit-bearing trees. Borams and tamarinds were my friend's constant companions—he even ate the seeds! Once, I joked, "Why don't you eat the mango seed?" He replied, "It won't come out," and I burst into laughter. He knew well enough that while Boram and tamarind seeds might pass through undigested, a mango seed was an entirely different challenge!

In a similar way, my friend knew that seeds won't be digested by his stomach, just as some things cannot be broken down by the land. Land pollution has a profound impact on plants, animals, and entire ecosystems. It leads to habitat destruction, biodiversity loss, and food chain contamination, destabilizing the natural balance and harming wildlife.

Plastic pollution has severe effects on both animals and plants, impacting ecosystems and biodiversity.

Land pollution, caused by the improper disposal of waste, chemicals, pesticides, and other harmful substances, has significant effects on plants and animals. Here's how it impacts both:

Toxic Test

As we have noticed, air pollution primarily damages leaves, while soil pollution presents a deeper challenge—one that begins at the roots. As plant roots drill into the soil, they encounter toxic tests in the form of hazardous chemicals, heavy metals, like lead, mercury, and cadmium, and pesticides. Plant growth is hindered, nutrient uptake reduced, and plant death may occur due to these pollutants.

Land degradation caused by pollution harms soil quality, impacting both wild plants and crops, thus reducing harvests. Contaminants are absorbed by plant roots, disrupting metabolism, growth, and reproduction. This creates an ecosystem-wide problem as animals consuming affected plants spread the toxins. Additionally, pollution from plastic waste and industrial residues damage the soil's physical structure, making it difficult for roots to penetrate. Landfill waste and heavy machinery compact soil thus reducing water absorption, restricting root growth, and weakening plant resilience.

Home and Bread

The figurative use of "home and bread" highlights the deprivation of shelter and food for fauna due to land pollution. It severely impacts wildlife by destroying habitats, contaminating the food chain, and introducing harmful substances into ecosystems. Deforestation, construction debris, and landfill waste strip animals of their natural shelters and food sources, forcing them to migrate or perish. As pollution seeps into the environment, it disrupts entire ecosystems, making survival increasingly difficult and threatening biodiversity. Habitat fragmentation makes survival increasingly difficult, leading to population decline. Additionally, pollutants absorbed by plants enter the food chain, causing bioaccumulation of toxic substances, like heavy metals and pesticides. This accumulation results in long-term health issues, reproductive failure, and even death, particularly for top predators.

Poisoning from industrial waste, pesticides, and chemicals in landfills further threatens animal health. Pollinators, like bees, suffer neurological damage, while birds and mammals experience reduced reproduction or fatal poisoning. Non-biodegradable waste, such as plastic, adds another layer of danger—animals mistake it for food, leading to digestive blockages, malnutrition, and death. Many also entangled in plastic waste, causing injuries or restricting movement, which often proves fatal.

As pollution degrades soil and vegetation, entire ecosystems are altered, impacting species that depend on them. Soil degradation affects invertebrates and insects, disrupting the food web and further endangering wildlife. The cascading effects of land pollution make it a critical threat to biodiversity and ecological balance.

Whistle

The whistle was a gift I received on one of my birthdays celebrated in Vancouver. I wondered—why a whistle? As a young boy, I had always admired bus conductors, who used whistles to halt buses, a practice still common in Goa. Curious, I gathered the courage to ask my benefactor, "Who told you that becoming a bus conductor was one of my childhood wishes?" She blinked in confusion and replied, "Sorry, I don't know what you're talking about."

"Oh! I thought that's why you gave me the whistle," I said. She laughed and clarified. "No, no. I gave it to you to chase away bears." Suddenly, it all made sense. Since I love hiking in the summer, the whistle was meant to frighten bears if we ever encountered them on our hikes. And what better place for adventure lovers than Vancouver? It is truly a cherry on top of the cake—a paradise for those who seek the thrill of the wild.

This reminded me of an account my grandmother once shared. She recalled how, when vehicles first arrived in villages, wild animals like foxes and leopards had disappeared. The sudden, unfamiliar noise had frightened them away, making them abandon their usual territories. Unusual sounds disrupt wildlife, triggering fear and forcing them to flee. Just as loud, unexpected noises drive animals away, noise pollution has far-reaching effects on both flora and fauna.

Victims of Noise

Humans often get thrilled by loud music and enjoy the energy of noise, but we fail to consider how this affects other creatures in our ecosystem. Flora and fauna becomes the victims of noise. Noise pollution, frequently underestimated, substantially impacts plants and animals by disrupting their natural functions and behaviors. Excessive noise pollution from traffic, industries, and urban development disrupts crucial animal communication. Consequently, species like birds, frogs, and marine life face more challenges in finding mates, escaping predators, and cooperating within their communities. The constant barrage of sound disrupts their way of life, making survival and reproduction more difficult.

Constant exposure to loud noise increases stress, leading to higher heart rates, weakened immune systems, hormonal imbalances, reduced lifespan, and lower reproductive success. Additionally, many species, such as birds and marine mammals, rely on natural sounds for navigation, and noise pollution can disorient them, disrupting migration routes and leading to habitat displacement. Prolonged exposure to loud noise can also cause hearing damage, altering animal behaviors and forcing them into less suitable habitats. The impact on plants is largely indirect but equally damaging. Noise pollution affects pollinators like bees and birds, reducing their efficiency in pollinating plants, which results in lower plant reproduction and biodiversity loss. It also disrupts seed dispersal as animals that aid in this process may be driven away by excessive noise, ultimately affecting plant growth and forest regeneration. Additionally, soil quality declines when noise pollution affects essential organisms, such as earthworms and insects, which contribute to soil aeration and nutrient cycling. A decrease in their activity can lead to degraded soil, negatively impacting plant health. Noise pollution is more than just an auditory disturbance; it disrupts entire ecosystems, threatening biodiversity and ecological balance. Mitigating its effects through conservation efforts, buffer zones, and controlled urban development is crucial for protecting wildlife and plant life.

The Red Flower

Years ago, the monsoon's arrival in Goa's lush, rain-drenched landscapes awakened a chorus of deep-throated frogs echoing through the misty fields and paddy lands. The calls attracting their mates also lured torch-bearing humans, skilled hunters, into the night's chase.

The simple yet clever trick was to shine a light directly into their gleaming eyes, instantly freezing the unsuspecting creatures in momentary blindness. A quick snatch and they were gone, their smooth bodies eluding grasps before meeting their end.

The next day, a fragrant masala would sizzle with prized frog legs, their tenderness filling kitchens with an irresistible aroma. Those privy to its delights anticipated a feast of a revered delicacy.

However, time has brought a change. The government banned the common practice after realizing the amphibians' crucial role in controlling the relentless mosquito swarms. Now, the wetlands' frog guardians sing their undisturbed songs, their melodies a seamless part of the monsoon symphony, untouched by human needs.

The relationship between creatures and light goes beyond the wetlands. I drew inspiration for the title *The Red Flower* from the movie *Mowgli*, where the animal kingdom refers to fire as the "red flower." Wild creatures feel both wonder and terror from the flickering flames' eerie glow. Its burning touch, insatiable hunger, and even its light fill them with fear—a force of both captivating and destructive power.

Typically, animals are drawn to the darkness, away from firelight, where nature's primal rhythm prevails. The unexpected flash of light, be it ancient firelight or modern glare, startles them in the stillness of night. Nocturnal beings, accustomed to the cloak of darkness, recoil at the intrusion, while even diurnal creatures, roused from their slumber, are left restless and disoriented. As blinding torchlight once trapped frogs, light similarly disrupts the fragile wild, wielding both power and danger.

Visual Alarm

For most of us, an audio alarm is our morning wake-up call. Animals and plants lack such devices, but artificial lights, our creation, similarly disturb them. I've named it visual alarm.

Excessive or wrongly directed artificial light at night, known as light pollution, seriously affects the natural cycles of plants and animals. Disrupted circadian rhythms affect wildlife's essential behaviors, including feeding, mating, and migration. The artificial brightness interferes with the lives of nocturnal creatures—bats, owls, and insects—while it causes disorientation and danger for migratory birds and sea turtles. Artificial light creates an imbalance, disrupting predator-prey relationships, thereby increasing vulnerability in some species, altering food chains and reducing biodiversity.

Artificial lights harm plants too. Natural growth cycles are disrupted, resulting in premature or delayed flowering and irregular leaf shedding. This disruption cascades through the ecosystem, especially harming nocturnal pollinators, such as moths and bats, whose plant interactions are vital for pollination. The desynchronization of these cycles initiates a chain reaction, weakening ecological stability and jeopardizing overall ecosystem health.

Just as a sudden beam of light once froze the frogs of Goa, artificial lights now disrupt the natural sleep cycle of the world. The natural world's delicate equilibrium, formerly guided by the sun, moon, and stars, is now unbalanced by artificial light, impacting countless species and fundamentally changing life.

Ocean, Fields, and Wind

In air pollution, we have touched on the thermal pollution, and in the land and water pollution, we have already talked about plastic. Here we will focus on some more information. Thermal pollution and plastic pollution are two pervasive environmental challenges that imperil the health of our ecosystems. Thermal pollution arises when industrial processes, power plants, or other human activities discharge heated water into natural water bodies, disrupting the delicate thermal balance essential for aquatic life. Elevated temperatures diminish dissolved oxygen levels and accelerate chemical reactions, stressing native species and undermining biodiversity. Meanwhile, plastic pollution, marked by the proliferation of plastic waste in oceans, rivers, and landscapes, presents a more visible yet equally destructive menace. Plastics, resistant to natural degradation, slowly break down into microplastics, which infiltrate the food chain, endangering marine life, terrestrial animals, and human health. Together, these forms of pollution not only compromise the natural rhythms of our planet but also underscore the urgent need for sustainable practices and robust environmental policies. Addressing both thermal and plastic pollution requires a concerted effort to innovate cleaner industrial methods, enforce stricter waste management protocols, and foster a global culture of conservation and responsibility.

Conclusion

Finally, while we've examined several main types of environmental pollution, it is vital to acknowledge that additional types—like radioactive, biological, and chemical pollutants—also devastate our planet. The chapter's purpose was to raise awareness of the damage these pollutants inflict on flora and fauna thereby upsetting the ecological equilibrium. Rather than providing an exhaustive account of every pollutant, the focus here has been on understanding how these harmful agents challenge the vitality of non-human life, all while human activities continue to be the prime drivers behind these environmental crises.

I FEEL I AM FREE

I feel I am free,
Yet someone else has built a prison for me.

I thought water was all I needed to swim,
But now the toxins, chemicals, and microplastics swim within.
It was never just water—and that is what choked us.
They call us free, yet through their actions, they imprison us.

I thought the sky was all I needed to fly,
But the noisy bits, the tangled wires, and fiber strings also occupy.
It was never just the sky—and that is what tore us.
They call us free, yet through their deeds, they destroy us.

I thought the land was all I needed to grow,
But now poison, plastic, and waste also sow
It was never just the land—and that is what asphyxiates us.
They call us free, yet through their waste, they devastate us.

I thought air was all I needed to breathe,
But now industries and vehicles spew poison beneath.
It was never just air—and that is what suffocates us.
They call us free, yet through their greed, they obliterate us.

I feel I am free,
Yet I pay the price for another's greed.

Chapter 6

Symptoms of Wounds

When talking about symptoms, we generally consider them as signals of an underlying problem. For instance, a warm body can be a symptom of a fever. However, when I speak of "symptoms of wounds," let us reverse the terms *wounds* to *symptoms*. Within this framework, the wounds are caused and its indication are its symptoms. It simply means symptoms of wounds on Mother Nature caused by human greed.

In a broader sense, human selfishness and disregard inflict deep wounds on nature, disrupting its delicate balance and harming both flora and fauna. Alarming wounds like global warming, climate change, food shortages, extinction, and other environmental calamities reveal these injuries. The gravity of these issues necessitates immediate action.

In this chapter, we explore the devastating impact of these environmental wounds and their far-reaching consequences. Global warming melts glaciers, raising sea levels and disrupting ecosystems reliant on glacial melt water. The displacement of wildlife grows as habitats shrink, leading to migration or extinction. Human activity negatively impacts birds by disrupting migration, depleting food, and introducing new dangers. Domestic animals aren't immune; they also face indigestion and other health issues from dirty water, diet changes, and pollutants. These linked symptoms are crucial warnings, demanding we recognize the severe environmental damage and act now to restore and protect our environment.

Change or Let Change

"Change or let change" is a striking and thought-provoking phrase that encapsulates a critical choice humanity faces: Either we change our indefensible practices and behaviors or allow climate change to force changes on us—likely in catastrophic and irreversible ways. This phrase serves as both a warning and a call to action, highlighting the urgency of addressing environmental and societal challenges. To set the tone, here are two quotes that align with this concept:

> "Twenty-five years ago people could be excused for not knowing much, or doing much, about climate change. Today we have no excuse."
> —Desmond Tutu, former archbishop of Cape Town

> "Climate change is the single greatest threat to a sustainable future but, at the same time, addressing the climate challenge presents a golden opportunity to promote prosperity, security and a brighter future for all."
> —Ban Ki-Moon, former secretary-general of the UN

Global warming and climate change are usually understood as interchangeable teams. However they have the distinct meanings.

Global warming is the long-term rise in earth's regular surface temperature caused by the accumulation of greenhouse gases, like carbon dioxide, methane, and nitrous oxide, in the atmosphere. It mainly focuses on earth's temperature, specifically its increase, particularly since the Industrial Revolution. Human actions, including burning fossil fuels, deforestation, and industry, release too many GHGs, which trap heat in the atmosphere and cause warming. Since the late nineteenth century, the earth's average temperature has risen by 1.1°C.

The term "climate change" describes the persistent fluctuations and changes in a region's or earth's characteristic weather patterns and climate. It covers a broad spectrum of changes, including precipitation, wind patterns, and the frequency of extreme weather events, not just temperature. Climate change refers to all modifications within the earth's climate system, encompassing warming, cooling, and alterations in precipitation and other atmospheric conditions. Although natural factors such as volcanic activity, solar radiation fluctuations, and natural cycles, like El Niño, can influence climate change, human-induced global warming is the most significant contributor.

For instance, "Climate change has led to increased severity of storms and droughts globally."

Human activities, especially the extensive use of fossil fuels, are responsible for these rapid changes. Coal, oil, and natural gas are all fossil fuels. The "greenhouse effect" in earth's atmosphere is a direct consequence of burning fossil fuels. The greenhouse effect occurs when sunlight is absorbed by the earth's surface and then released as heat. Certain atmospheric gases act like a blanket, trapping heat around earth. Fossil fuel combustion releases gasses that effectively trap heat, hindering their escape from the atmosphere. These greenhouse gasses are carbon dioxide, methane, nitrous oxide, chlorofluorocarbons, and water vapor. The earth's temperature has risen over time because of the excess heat in the atmosphere, a phenomenon called global warming.

For example the Industrial Revolution, which started in the mid-eighteenth century, triggered a human-caused increase in greenhouse gas emissions originating in Europe and the United States. With the invention of the coal-fired steam engine, coal emerged as a significant energy source. It quickly became a source of heat for homes and power for factories.

The use of fossil fuels has been steadily increasing since that point. Fossil fuels are a key source of energy for power generation, heating, and transportation in numerous countries today. Emissions of greenhouse gasses have skyrocketed in the last hundred years and especially since the 1980s. Earth's temperature has increased faster because of this.

Global warming has presented humans with this issue: climate change. Global warming causes climate change, which poses a serious threat to life on earth.

Climate change, driven by global warming, is causing severe droughts, wildfires, and extreme storms with heavier rainfall, impacting people across the globe. Higher temperatures are altering ecosystems, forcing animals to migrate to cooler places to survive. Unless global temperatures are reduced, scientists warn that numerous species will face extinction.

Ocean temperatures are rising, causing glaciers, ice caps, and ice sheets to melt. This is causing sea levels to rise, creating flooding problems for many people who live on islands and in coastal communities.

Nations worldwide are working to decrease greenhouse gas emissions to combat global warming. The Paris Agreement was signed by almost two hundred nations at a UN Climate Change conference held in 2015. The international treaty requires every country to reduce greenhouse gas emissions. The aim is to curb global warming and stop earth's temperature from increasing by 2°C (3.6°F) above preindustrial levels. Here below let us have a look at the aftermath of human inference on nature—in other words the symptoms of wounds inflected by human on flora and fauna.

Kedarnath

Kedarnath, India: spiritual and scenic marvel, Kedarnath, located in Uttarakhand's Rudraprayag District, is a sacred town located at 3,583 meters (11,755 feet) in the Garhwal Himalayas. Renowned for the Kedarnath Temple, a revered shrine of Lord Shiva, and one of the twelve Jyotirlingas, it is surrounded by snow-clad peaks, including the towering Kedarnath Mountain (6,940 meters). A destination of faith and natural beauty, it attracts millions of pilgrims and adventurers, making it one of India's most iconic sites.

Here is the story of a pilgrimage shared with BBC One on June9, 2013: The pilgrim embarked on a journey to Kedarnath with his wife, Chhota Devi, two brothers, their wives, and another relative. Having already visited Badrinath, Yamunotri, and Gangotri, this trip was meant to complete their Char Dham Yatra.

"Kedarnath was the only one left," he recalled.

On June16, the group reached the Kedarnath temple, a moment of spiritual fulfillment. After offering prayers, they began their descent to Rambara, a small village to rest. However, heavy rain greeted them during the trek.

By 5:00 p.m., they reached Rambara, where they decided to spend the night.

That night, the serenity of chanting Lord Ram's name by the Alaknanda

River was shattered by ominous noises. "It felt like the mountain began to tremble. Huge boulders started rolling down, sweeping people into the river," he recounted. In the pitch-dark chaos, he saw his wife, sister-in-law, and elder brother swept away. Unable to locate the others, he found refuge by clinging to a large boulder. Observing the destruction, he noticed hills with trees fared better than the barren, rocky ones. He climbed a tree and clung to its branches for survival.

"From a distance, I saw an entire mountain dissolve into the river. My mind went numb."

For four days, he endured freezing conditions, starvation, and injuries. Despite dislocating his shoulder, he put it back into place. Around him, others succumbed to the cold and dehydration.

With no communication or hope of rescue, he resigned himself to fate, clinging to faith.

On June 20, a rescue helicopter arrived, evacuating survivors to Guptkashi and later to Dehradun. He was hospitalized, his body weakened and his skin peeling from prolonged exposure. The realization of his survival brought mixed emotions. While his children rejoiced at his return, they struggled to accept the loss of their mother and relatives.

"The bodies were never found. Initially, my children hoped their mother might return, but they eventually accepted the reality."

Despite the trauma, his devotion remains unshaken. "Would I go to Kedarnath again? Yes, emphatically yes. There is no point in living with fear." He even wishes to take his children on the pilgrimage, affirming his belief in facing life without fear.

This survivor's account is a poignant reminder of human resilience and faith amid unimaginable loss.

The Kedarnath flood of 2013 was a devastating disaster caused by a combination of natural and human-induced factors. In June 2013, the region experienced exceptionally heavy rainfall—about 375 percent above normal levels—due to an unusual interaction between the monsoon system and a Western disturbance. Rising global temperatures accelerated the retreat of Himalayan glaciers, contributing to erratic weather patterns and increased glacial melt. The melting of the Chorabari Glacier significantly raised water levels in Chorabari Lake, located upstream of Kedarnath. Continuous rainfall and glacial melt caused the lake to breach, resulting in a glacial lake outburst flood (GLOF), which released massive volumes of water and debris, inundating Kedarnath and its surroundings. The melting of glaciers effects are illustrated by the example of Kedarnath.

The Glacial Lake Outburst Flood in Bhutan (1994), the Uttarakhand Floods in India (2021), the collapse of the Larsen B Ice Shelf in Antarctica (2002), and many more events, illustrates this concept.

We should examine the scientific research on this crucial matter more closely. The GRACE (Gravity Recovery and Climate Experiment) mission, launched in March 2002 and concluding in June 2017, was a collaborative initiative between NASA and the German Aerospace Center (DLR). GRACE's use of twin satellites to measure variations in earth's gravity field enabled the collection of critical data about shifts in mass distribution across the planet. This included important findings regarding melting ice sheets, rising sea levels, groundwater depletion, and other topics. Though GRACE was primarily designed to measure earth's gravity-field variations, its data has also significantly helped us understand climate-related processes.

One of GRACE's most significant contributions to climate science is the ability to measure the loss of ice in Greenland, Antarctica, and other glaciated regions. The data showed that ice is melting at an increasing rate due to rising global temperatures, significantly contributing to rising sea levels. Melting glaciers, shrinking ice sheets, and warmer water expanding all contributed to changes in ocean mass, as observed by GRACE. These measurements allowed scientists to quantify the contributions of various sources to sea-level rise.

GRACE's monitoring of water mass distribution also revealed the effects of climate change on the global water cycle, such as changes in rainfall patterns, worsening droughts, and variations in freshwater storage. This is particularly significant because the Greenland and Antarctic ice sheets hold about two-thirds of earths fresh water. The melting of glaciers and ice sheets, primarily due to rising temperatures on earth's surface and in its oceans, has caused roughly one-third of the global average sea level rise since 1993. These findings underline the importance of continued scientific efforts to understand and address climate change.

Let's use Ms. Kathy Jetnil-Kijiner's powerful poem to understand climate change's reality. Representing the Marshall Islands' civil society, she read this moving piece at the UN Climate Summit's 2014 opening. Addressing her infant daughter, Matafele Peinam, the poem vividly describes a tender yet perilous reality. Let's take a look at some lines from the poem, "Dear Matafele Peinam."

> Dear matafele peinam ... don't cry mommy promises young one
> will come and devour you
> no greedy whale of a company sharking through political seas
> no backwater bullying of businesses with broken morals
> no blindfolded bureaucracies gonna push
> this mother ocean over the edge on one's drowning, baby
> no one's moving
> no one's losing their home land no one's gonna become a climate change refugee...

The poem, "Dear Matafele Peinam," begins with a tender, loving tone as a mother describes her baby daughter with affectionate imagery, highlighting the innocence and joy of childhood in their island home. As the poem progresses, the tone shifts to urgency and fear, warning of the threat of climate change and rising sea levels, which could destroy their land and displace future generations.

Despite these fears, the speaker refuses to accept a future of loss. She vows to protect her daughter and her homeland, declaring resistance against powerful corporations and governments that contribute to climate destruction. The poem acknowledges the suffering of island communities already affected and calls for solidarity and action.

It then expands to a hopeful vision of global activism—showing people from all walks of life uniting to fight for environmental justice. In the end, the poem returns to a peaceful and intimate tone as the mother reassures her child that she will be safe, leaving the reader with a strong sense of hope, determination, and the promise of a better future.

You Encroached

A neighbor shared a striking story with me during a discussion about the effects of human activity on wildlife. The air vibrated with the song of cicadas on a sunny summer day, when a middle-aged couple stumbled on the peaceful ferocity of nature.

The wife, standing outside their country home, confronted her husband with sharp words and crossed arms. "You encroached," she declared, her words cutting through the stillness like a blade.

Her accusation stemmed from the husband's impulsive decision the day before. The blazing heat inspired him to build a swimming pool on the edge of their property, near the old well. It seemed like an ideal plan—unlimited water from the well and a motor pump to realize his dream. Wasting no time, he grabbed an axe and sickle and cleared a patch of land, felling a small grove of trees in the process.

He had no idea those trees were sheltering a dangerous Indian cobra. The serpent, its shimmering black scales now vulnerable to the scorching summer sun, was driven out into the open by the sudden destruction of its home.

The following morning, as the couple prepared for breakfast, the wife let out a piercing scream. She saw a cobra coiled on their doorstep, its hood flared, issuing a silent but unmistakable warning.

Startled, the husband scrambled for a nearby wooden log. Unshakeable, the cobra let out a quiet hiss, its forked tongue moving rapidly, resembling a flame. With trembling hands, he raised the log, ready to strike.

"You intruder!" he barked, his voice laced more with fear than anger.

Before he could act, his wife's voice rang out again, sharp and accusatory, "You encroached first!"

Her words hung heavy in the air, stopping him in his tracks. The weight of the truth in her statement made him falter. The cobra, as if aware of the change, dropped its hood, fixing its intense stare on the man.

He carefully lowered the log and then moved away. The couple watched in silence as the cobra uncoiled itself and slithered away, retreating into the shadows of their garage. A snake catcher arrived within the hour, safely relocating the serpent and preventing further harm.

As they stood in the aftermath of the encounter, the wife turned to her husband, her tone softer but firm. "You disrupted its world for your dream. Consider the impact of your actions before taking something from another person or thing.

The husband, visibly chastened, nodded in quiet agreement. Despite the intense sun beating down on their land, a clear message emerged: Every trespass has its price.

This is only one of countless such incidents. The same tales are told in villages throughout the region. Villagers frequently complain about the growing monkey menace as large groups of monkeys jump on roofs and damage tiles. Their raids on gardens and orchards are born of desperation—a scarcity of fruiting trees in the forests forces them into human settlements.

On national highways, another tragedy unfolds. As forests shrink and migration corridors are obliterated, wild animals wander into traffic, leading to frequent and often fatal accidents. Every instance serves as a stark reminder of the fragile balance we upset when we intrude on nature.

Nature, in its quiet and unforgiving way, always responds. Maybe it's time we pay attention to the warnings it's sending and reevaluate how we treat our planet.

Nightmare at a Festival

Celebrations are enjoyable for everyone, aren't they? Celebrations are an intrinsic part of human life. Our emotions surge when excitement takes over. Actions and words are common outlets for these emotions. This excitement is fantastic, but exceeding boundaries or upsetting people leads to trouble.

For numerous immigrant families, Canada is a land of opportunity, a diverse nation with a rich tapestry of cultures and ethnicities. A friend of mine shared an incident that highlights how cultural festivities can sometimes clash with societal norms.

On one occasion, an ethnic group was celebrating their traditional feast with great pomp at the home of one of the participants. Following a sumptuous meal, around nine at night, the group exited to partake in some party games. A neighbor illuminated their courtyard around ten thirty.

For the celebrators, this seemed like a gesture of participation or solidarity. However, for the neighbors, it was a silent warning to quiet down.

Fifteen minutes later, the police arrived, effectively ending the festivities. A noise complaint had been filed by the neighbors. However, there was speculation that this complaint stemmed from a lingering grudge due to a past disagreement.

Regardless of the cause, this incident reveals a more significant problem. We humans are often so focused on our own comfort and well-being that we sometimes disregard the impact of our actions on others, including animals and birds, who cannot voice their discomfort. This principle covers all pollution, not just noise pollution.

While celebrations are lovely, it's important to be thoughtful of everyone and everything around us, from humans to animals.

Fireworks inflict physical and behavioral harm on birds, resulting in substantial stress and potential injury. Loud noises and bright flashes frequently surprise and confuse birds, causing a "fight or flight" response. This stress is heightened in urban and suburban areas, where fireworks are more frequent and chronic stress can weaken a bird's immune system, making them more prone to disease. The nocturnal nature of fireworks clashes with birds' sleep, resulting in fatigue, compromised immunity, and reduced foraging success the following day. The disturbances can also cause birds to abandon their nests or roosting sites, particularly during breeding seasons, when eggs or chicks may be left behind. Erratic flight in panicked birds can lead to collisions with obstacles like buildings, trees, and power lines, resulting in injuries or fatalities. Some birds, in their desperate attempts to escape, may venture into dangerous areas like highways, increasing the risk of fatal accidents. Sudden lights and noises easily disrupt the navigation of migratory birds, leading to them to fly off course and become exhausted from pointless detours, thus increasing their vulnerability. These cumulative effects underscore the need to consider wildlife when planning firework displays.

These are some of the effects of noise pollution on birds. Nevertheless, we don't have to abandon fireworks entirely. The spectacular display of lights in the sky is undeniably captivating and admired by many. To minimize harm to wildlife, it would be ideal to hold such events in open fields far from trees and areas where birds are known to nest or roost.

Careful location choices let us celebrate while respecting the environment and its creatures.

The nightmare of feasts makes me think of Makar Sankranti. Celebrated January 14, Makar Sankranti signals the height of festivities beginning mid-December across much of northern and western India. A vibrant tradition of kite flying accompanies this festival, with colorful kites made of lightweight paper and bamboo filling the skies. This joyous activity often turns competitive as participants use abrasive-coated strings, such as those embedded with glass powder, to cut down opponents' kites. Ahmedabad (Gujarat) and Jaipur (Rajasthan) host renowned kite festivals, attracting kite lovers worldwide. Makar Sankranti is known for kite flying, but India's Independence Day in August includes similar popular celebrations.

However, the dense web of kite strings during these festivals poses a severe threat to birds, turning the skies into a hazardous trap. Frequent victims of collisions include pigeons, kites, parrots, and critically endangered birds, like vultures, many sustaining serious harm. Razor-sharp Chinese nylon thread, prohibited in India as of 2017, significantly intensified the issue. Despite the ban, conservation organizations continue to rescue thousands of injured birds every year. In 2018, for instance, the Gujarat state forest department successfully rescued over four thousand birds post-Makar Sankranti. Recent efforts to promote the use of cotton threads have somewhat reduced the severity of injuries, offering a glimmer of hope for safer celebrations in the future.

Report Card Adventure

My older sister's recollection of this incident would be far superior to mine, as I was joyous, while she was petrified. This happened over Diwali break, just after my midterm exams. While my siblings, attended secondary school in the mornings, I went to primary school in the evenings.

At that time, I hadn't yet learned to ride a bicycle, but my eldest sister was a pro. During the holidays, one specific day was set aside for collecting report cards, and the condition was that a guardian or someone older had to accompany us. To get my report card, my sister, a cycling enthusiast, offered to come along.

We set out in the midday sun, which was so harsh it erased our shadows and drenched my sister in sweat as she pedaled. Meanwhile, I sat on the rear bracket, merrily singing and enjoying the gentle breeze. Reaching the school, my classroom was our next destination.

The teacher began her usual litany, "Cannio can study, but he does not study..." and continued her complaints. My sister, a former student of the same teacher, stared with silent disdain, her own past mirrored in the present. Once we were done, we stepped out into the sweltering heat with parched throats.

Our school was not fenced back then, and stray cows often roamed around the enormous concrete garbage bins nearby, scavenging for food. Because of the summer's lack of grass, the cows were drawn to the bins.

My sister darted to the bicycle, while I insisted on stopping to drink water at the tap section on the school campus. She put the report card onto the bracket of the bike. It wasn't her delay but mine—I lingered, imitating a local soccer player by keeping my head under the tap. Now, I was drenched, not with sweat but with water. Despite being annoyed with me, she still wiped my face with her handkerchief. But as we returned, we were stunned to see bike toppled over, and a stray cow munching my report card!

I was thrilled—overjoyed, even. The cow had eaten the evidence of my poor marks! My sister, on the other hand, broke out in a cold sweat. She was almost in tears, while I couldn't stop giggling. "No report card equals no scolding from Mama!" I declared triumphantly.

Though this incident makes us laugh now, it brings to light a critical issue: the plight of stray animals. Below are a few examples.

Searching for food, stray cows frequently eat plastic bags near rubbish dumps in numerous cities. A 2017 Delhi study found an average of twenty-five kilograms of plastic in the stomachs of many deceased cows. Similarly, in Nairobi, Kenya, veterinarians once operated on a cow and removed nearly twenty kilograms of plastic waste, including polythene bags. A cow in Sri Lanka was found to have over forty kilograms of plastic in its stomach after a postmortem.

This issue isn't limited to cows; it affects other animals too. A tragic example is a four-hundred-pound black bear in the US that was euthanized after consuming a significant amount of human garbage, including plastic wrappers and paper products. Severe intestinal decay, caused by a blockage, left the bear in excruciating pain, paralyzed, and exhibiting symptoms, including eye discharge.

If we, as humans, suffer immensely from stomach pain when we eat something wrong, imagine the plight of animals who cannot discern what they're consuming. Our failure to sort our waste endangers these innocent animals.

Let's own this. Protecting our planet and its inhabitants requires responsible waste management and less plastic use.

Conclusion

The earth it talking to us, but we are not listing. Yes, the damage we've done to nature is profound, and the plants and animals are paying the price. It's crucial we recognize the damage done and take responsibility for raising awareness. However, awareness alone is not enough; we must also take proactive steps to heal the environment by carefully analyzing the symptoms of its distress. For example, animal displacement clearly shows deforestation since their homes are lost to human development. We can restore ecological balance and shelter displaced wildlife by conserving existing forests, strengthening conservation laws, and actively planting trees. Planting trees and cutting pollution, even in small ways, aids nature's healing and renewal. The time to act is now—our collective responsibility is to not only recognize the wounds but also work tirelessly toward their cure. We have to open our eyes before it is too late.

THE EARTH

The earth once flourished, so green, so wide,
With rivers that gushed and oceans with tide.
The woods would whisper, the hills would sing,
A harmony of life in a never-ending spring.

But now the air is misty and literally ill,
Smoke from the industries, a bitter pill.
The glaciers lament as they melt away,
The sea elevates with each passing day.

The forests burn, the flora flee,
A scar on the fauna, a tragedy.
The sky turns gloomy, the earth turns dry,
And nature watches with a somber sigh.

Oceans are pungent, filled with despair,
Plastic and waste hover everywhere.
Coral reefs, once stunning and bright,
Now fade to dimness, losing their light.

The sun piracies down, fierce and unkind
As if grilling the whole living kind.
Storms grow healthier, floods invade,
A price we pay for the choices we trade.

But there is hope, if only we try,
To heal the earth, to dry her eye.
Plant the trees, clean the seas,
And provide the fresh air to set hearts at ease.

We have the power, we seize the key,
To shape the future, to set her free.
Let's act today, sooner than it's too late,
And rephrase tomorrow, with love, not hate.

For earth is not ours to annihilate or consume
But a home to treasure, to let life bloom.
So rise, my dear, and make a stand,
Together we can heal this land.

Chapter 7

Mastermind

God is the mastermind behind the creation of all things—a divine intelligence who upholds the equilibrium of Mother Earth, nurturing the growth and sustenance of all living creatures. A divine power responsible for creation and preservation of all flora and fauna is a belief system common across numerous religions and their scriptures.

Key religious texts reveal profound insights into the spiritual bond between the divine and nature. This concept underscores the sacred trust bestowed on humanity—God entrusted this creation to human beings, granting them the responsibility to lead, nurture, and safeguard it.

Divine Intelligence

The Zixo puzzle can be seen as a metaphor for the intricate design and profound intelligence behind the natural world. A puzzle piece corresponds to each existential element. Like nature's balanced harmony, these pieces reveal a larger picture when properly assembled.

The concept of divine intelligence designing this puzzle suggests that a higher power has intricately planned and arranged every piece with precision. The design's unity is achieved through each piece's distinct place and contribution. The placement of these pieces isn't random; it reflects a thoughtful and deliberate orchestration that ensures the beauty and functionality of the final image.

Similar to a puzzle needing all its pieces, the universe needs each part to fulfill its purpose for wholeness. This analogy highlights the idea of interconnection and purpose in life. Furthermore, the process of solving the Zixo puzzle mirrors humanity's journey of discovery and understanding. It requires patience, insight, and alignment with the greater design to bring the scattered pieces together.

The complexity and precision of nature implies a conscious force behind it. Consider the mind-boggling array of plants and animals, each perfectly adapted to their own environment, reveals intricate craftsmanship. From flower's delicate symmetry to animals' complex social structures, such design suggests intelligence and planning. Nature's symbiotic relationships, such as those between pollinators and plants or predators and prey, create a balanced and harmonious ecosystem vital for survival. This fits the notion of a divine being who is both creator and giver of purpose, resulting in a unified cosmos.

Nature's beautiful diversity would show a god's boundless creativity. Flowers' bright colors, trees' towering presence, and plant life's range—from microscopic algae to ancient sequoias—might be seen as art created by a divine being. The creative force celebrating diversity is revealed through animals' varied forms, abilities, and behaviors. A butterfly's vibrant patterns, a lion's strength, and a deer's grace all demonstrate intentional design .Life, as designed by this god, inherently inspires awe and reverence through its creative nature. This is beautifully articulated by St. Basil (329–379) "I want creation to penetrate you with so much admiration that wherever you go, the least plant may bring you clear remembrance of the Creator. A single plant, a blade of grass, or one speck of dust is sufficient to occupy all your intelligence in beholding the art with which it has been made."

A powerful, all-knowing being would not just create but also uphold life's complex systems. This position demands foresight into the needs of living things and the creation of natural laws to ensure equilibrium. For instance, rainfall, thanks to the water cycle and the change of seasons, respectively provides water for and regulates the growth and reproduction of plants. Ecological succession and adaptation systems allow life to rebound and develop despite obstacles, mirroring a deity's foresight and nurture.

Creation and this divine being are fundamentally interwoven, their existence is inseparable. Across various belief systems, the divine is considered present in the natural world, with the life energy in all creatures potentially representing God's spirit. God's continues presence and actions in the world could be symbolized by natural cycles, such as seasonal changes and the cycle of life and death. A divine being, actively participating in life's interconnectedness, is evoked by this view, a being of both transcendence and immanence.

Six Days

The Bible, the holy book of Christians, provides a clear account of God's creation in the book of Genesis, describing how the world was formed in six days. The Bible, emphasizing God's wisdom and power, describes plants and animals as key components of the systematic creation of all living things.

In Genesis 1:11–12, it is written, "And God said, 'Let the earth put forth vegetation, plants yielding seed, and fruit trees bearing fruit in which is their seed, each according to its kind, upon the earth.' And it was so. The earth brought forth vegetation, plants yielding seed according to their own kinds, and trees bearing fruit in which is their seed, each according to its kind. And God saw that it was good."

Similarly, Genesis 1:20–25 states, "And God said, 'Let the waters bring forth swarms of living creatures, and let birds fly above the earth across the firmament of the heavens.' So God created the great sea monsters and every living creature that moves, with which the waters swarm, according to their kinds, and every winged bird according to its kind. And God saw that it was good. And God blessed them, saying, 'Be fruitful and multiply and fill the waters in the seas, and let birds multiply on the earth.' And there was evening and there was morning, a fifth day.

And God said, 'Let the earth bring forth living creatures according to their kinds: cattle and creeping things and beasts of the earth according to their kinds.' And it was so. And God made the beasts of the earth according to their kinds and the cattle according to their kinds, and everything that creeps upon the ground according to its kind. And God saw that it was good."

These passages depict God as a meticulous designer, ensuring balance, order, and diversity in nature. They highlight divine wisdom as the driving force behind the variety of life.

Humanity, crowned by God as the pinnacle of creation, received intellect and the responsibility for caring for the earth and its inhabitants. As stated in Genesis 2:15, "The Lord God took the man and put him in the Garden of Eden to work it and take care of it."

While humans were given dominion over animals, this translates to responsible care, not abuse. Genesis 1:28 declares, "Rule over the fish of the sea and the birds of the air and every creature that crawls upon the earth."

Moreover, Matthew 6:26 reminds believers of God's provision for all living beings: "Look at the birds of the air; they do not sow or reap or store away in barns, and yet your heavenly Father feeds them."

Christian belief sees plants and animals as God's deliberate creations, highlighting His magnificence, inventiveness, and loving care. From plants and animals, we get sustenance, beauty, and a glimpse of God's magnificence. Protecting creation's diverse harmony is humanity's role as stewards. God's intentional design and boundless love are revealed in the interdependence of plants and animals.

Let's consider the great Catholic saint, St. Francis of Assisi (AD 1181–1226), as an example to end this section. As the patron saint of animals, he's famous for his deep care and concern for them. Nevertheless, his solitude was, as shown, an illusion. Many earlier saints, especially those living solitary and ascetic lives, displayed compassion for animals, echoing humanity's original, Edenic state of peaceful coexistence with nature.

St. Francis, known for preaching to animals, reportedly negotiated a peace treaty between a wolf terrorizing Gubbio and its people, securing the wolf's food supply in return for an end to violence. A revolutionary for his era, Francis abandoned the traditional monastic life to establish a band of traveling preachers, receiving the Pope's blessing in 1209.

Francis saw the divine in everything natural—the sun, moon, mountains, wind, water, and animals. He called all of creation his siblings, referring to the sun as "Brother Sun" and the moon as "Sister Moon."

In zest Christianity, God is viewed as the Creator and Sustainer of all flora and fauna. Humans are regarded as the crown of creation and entrusted with the role of stewards, responsible for caring for and preserving the natural world.

Allah's

The Quran describes God (Allah) as the ultimate Creator of the universe and everything within it. His role as the Creator is central to the Islamic understanding of existence, highlighting His omnipotence, knowledge, and ability to bring all things into being from nothing. Islam views the creation of plants and animals as powerful evidence of Allah's might, wisdom, and compassion. The Quran highlights Allah's meticulous design in all of creation, emphasizing the deliberate nature of life, from plants to animals.

Quran 39:62 states, "Allah is the Creator of all things, and He is, over all things, Disposer of affairs."

The Quran often inspires believers to ponder the miracles of creation. For Instance, "Do they not ever reflect on camels—how they were masterfully created; and the sky—how it was raised high; and the mountains—how they were firmly set up; and the earth—how it was leveled out?"*(Quran 88:17–20)*.

Additionally, Quran 7:54 states, "Indeed, your Lord is Allah, Who created the heavens and the earth in six Days, then established Himself on the Throne. He makes the day and night overlap in rapid succession. He created the sun, the moon, and the stars—all subjected by His command. The creation and the command belong to Him alone. Blessed is Allah—Lord of all worlds!"

The Quran, specifically in Surah An-Nahl (16:10–11), demonstrates the interconnectedness of life: "He is the One Who sends down rain from the sky, from which you drink and by which plants grow for your cattle to graze."

These verses stress the detail in Allah's creation, the interconnectedness of nature, and the thoughtful design behind it.

Islam emphasizes the importance of kindness and compassion toward animals, acknowledging their unique roles within God's creation. This is a theme emphasized by the Prophet Muhammad (peace be on him) in various teachings. For Example, "Whoever is kind to the creatures of Allah is kind to himself" (Hadith).

Examples from the Hadith, including a woman's pardon for giving a thirsty dog water and another's condemnation for neglecting a cat, underscore the importance of looking after animals. These teachings emphasize the moral imperative to treat animals with kindness and consideration.

The Quran encourages Muslims to ponder creation's signs, acknowledging Allah's balanced work. Plants and animals serve as reminders of the interconnectedness of life and as sources of sustenance and reflection. Human responsibility for appreciating, respecting, and protecting all life is central to the concept of environmental stewardship.

Islamic teachings, including scriptures and the Prophet Muhammad's lessons, present a vision where humans, as earth's caretakers, are responsible for protecting Allah's other creations.

Brahma

In Hinduism, the origin of plants and animals is intrinsically linked to its cosmology, mythology, and philosophy. This creation reflects divine will and energy, representing the unity and interdependence of life. Plants and animals, seen as sacred embodiments of the divine, are essential to cosmic balance (Dharma).

In Hindu scriptures, the creation and sustenance of life are attributed to deities, for instance: Brahma, the Creator, is responsible for the creation of all living beings. Vishnu, the Protector, ensures life's continuity. Devi embodies the nurturing essence of nature.

The Bhagavad Gita (chapter 10, verse 8) declares, "I am the source of all spiritual and material worlds. Everything emanates from Me. The wise who know this perfectly engage in My devotional service and worship Me with all their hearts."

This verse positions the divine as both the origin and sustainer of life. Hindu texts describe the emergence of life as arising from the five great elements (*pancha mahabhutas*): earth, water, fire, air, and space. From Brahma's mind and body emanated all creatures, including plants, animals, and humans, each fulfilling a role in the cosmic order.

Hinduism stresses compassion and nonviolence (ahimsa) toward all life, deeply respecting nature. Plants are especially revered as sustenance and divine embodiments. Associated with Goddess Lakshmi and Lord

Vishnu, Tulsi (Holy Basil) is considered a purifier and protector. People view it as the sacred dividing line between heaven and earth.

Animals are integral to the cosmic order and often hold religious significance. As a sacred symbol of motherhood and abundance, the cow is connected to the wish-fulfilling Kamadhenu. People deeply respect the cow, considering it a divine gift that sustains all life.

Hinduism teaches that plants, animals, and humans are interdependent, and their relationship is key to nature's equilibrium. As stated in the Bhagavad Gita (3:14), "All beings arise from food, and food arises from plants. Plants grow because of rain, and rain is a gift of the divine." Preserving flora and fauna is essential for upholding Dharma, the cosmic order.

Hindu philosophy teaches that all living beings have a soul (atman) and are connected to the divine essence (Brahman). This understanding fosters respect for all forms of life. Ahimsa (nonviolence) promotes compassion and refraining from violence, acknowledging the inherent worth of all life. Plants and animals are included in the cycle of birth and rebirth, known as samsara. Your actions and how you treat others determine your karma and affect your spiritual journey.

In Hinduism, the divine creation of plants and animals is viewed as a sacred act, symbolizing the interconnectedness of all living things. Plants and animals represent more than just food; they embody spiritual meaning and carry divine energy. A harmonious relationship between humanity and the environment is promoted in Hindu philosophy through the reverence of nature.

Nāstika

While our conversations concentrate on the divine's creative role, Jainism provides a different perspective on existence, stressing natural laws and eternal truths. Because it's a Nāstika tradition (na, "not," and āstika, "believing in"), Jainism doesn't believe in a creator deity or a divine creation. Rather, it claims the universe and everything in it is eternal, self-regulating, and subject to unchanging laws.

Jainism, unlike many other religions, doesn't credit a god with creating the universe, plants, or animals. Rather, it posits an eternal, self-existent universe governed by natural laws, lacking a beginning or end. This viewpoint applies to all living creatures, such as plants and animals.

Jainism's core principles of non-violence, respect for all life, and the cosmos's self-sustaining nature underpin its distinctive view of plants and animals.

Jainism teaches that every living thing, from plants to people, has an inherently pure and eternal soul (jiva). A being's actions create karmic bonds, shaping its future existence. Plants and animals, along with all other living things, share the quality of consciousness, although the extent of their consciousness may differ. Single-Sensed Beings (Ekendriya) are organisms, such as plants and microorganisms, that can feel. Multi-Sensed Beings (Bahusvara) consist of animals, humans, and superior life forms that have various senses, like touch, taste, sight, hearing, and smell.

Jainism advocates complete non violence toward plants. Although plants serve as sustenance for Jains, they are urged to minimize harm during harvesting, ensuring plants aren't uprooted or destroyed. Root vegetables such as onions, garlic, and potatoes are avoided since harvesting them destroys the plant and disrupts soil microorganisms. Animals possess multiple senses and varying degrees of awareness. These creatures feel complex emotions and pain and are vital to their ecosystems.

I have mentioned Jainism in this section, even though it does not believe in God; however, it holds great reverence for flora and fauna. Understanding these diverse religious views enriches our appreciation of different spiritual and ethical approaches to nature, fostering greater respect for environmental responsibility across traditions.

Restoring and Storing

> The time for seeking global solutions is
> running out. We can find suitable solutions
> only if we act together and in agreement.
> —Pope Francis

Let's explore collaborative methods for the restoration and preservation of our world in this section. We'll also showcase examples of proactive individuals; proving collective action with shared goals can create meaningful change.

Recently, I read about Jadav Payeng, also known as the "Forest Man of India."

Majuli, nestled in the Brahmaputra River in Assam, India, is the largest river island in the world. However, years of soil erosion have destroyed its banks, causing the loss of numerous nearby islands. There are now fears that Majuli may also be lost.

Across India, the landscape is changing dramatically, largely due to climate change. It's a bleak reality for the people of Majuli and nearby Jorhat, Jadav's hometown.

Jadav's childhood was filled with forest adventures. However, one day he stumbled on a horrifying scene: Dead snakes littered Majuli's shores, casualties of the island's arid landscape. He felt something stir within him at that moment. Sixteen-year-old Jadav's life was altered by his decision to begin planting trees.

Initially, progress was slow. Driven by instinct, he planted a diverse range of seeds, understanding the importance of biodiversity. However, large parts of the island consisted of barren sandbars, making seed-finding difficult. With determination, Jadav journeyed great distances to gather seeds, transporting them back to Majuli.

Once the trees were mature and producing their own seeds, the process became self-sustaining. In the following four decades, Jadav's tree-planting efforts converted 1,400 acres of land, resulting in over 1.5 million trees.

"I've planted every tree by myself," Jadav says.

Jadav's work is striking because he didn't seek recognition. His work remained unrecognized for decades. Then, during 2008, his forest received a visit from a herd of elephants. Following the elephants, wildlife officials were astonished to find a flourishing forest where there used to be barren sandbars.

Today, Majuli offers refuge to elephants, deers, tigers, rabbits, monkeys, birds, reptiles, and many awestruck visitors. Jadav's story has captivated scientists, journalists, and filmmakers.

Jadav Payeng is rightly celebrated as a hero in India and around the world. Reforestation and regeneration are, according to his work, vital in the battle against climate change.

This recounts the tale of a man who cultivated a whole forest. Imagine the possibilities if everyone contributed, in any way they could, to a greener planet.

German environmental activist Felix Finkbeiner's Plant-for-the-Planet organization has planted over 14 billion trees, a journey that started when he was nine.

Addressing the UN General Assembly as a child, Finkbeiner criticized adults for failing to act on climate change, warning that his generation would bear the brunt of their inaction. His inspiration led him to create Plant-for-the-Planet, a global reforestation and climate awareness movement.

In collaboration with the UN's Billion Tree Campaign, Finkbeiner's goal expanded to planting a trillion trees—150 per person globally. In addition to reforestation, the organization fosters young climate leaders, advocates for sustainability, and demands accountability from those in power.

Through its tree-planting app, Plant-for-the-Planet connects people and companies to support global reforestation, revitalizing degraded areas and fostering sustainable employment.

"Each tree is a symbol of hope," Finkbeiner says. "Together, they represent a tangible solution to a pressing global problem."

Today, Felix Finkbeiner's influence on the environment as a young activist is widely celebrated. His work's impact includes inspiring millions to act and showcasing the power of youth in global change.

Finkbeiner's commitment demonstrates that impactful environmental work transcends age. His journey toward a trillion trees showcases the power within us all to create a more equitable, healthy, and environmentally conscious world.

Despite living in cities where we may not have large properties to plant trees, we can still help protect and nurture flora. Look for an opportunity to join in finding meaningful ways to support plant well-being in our urban setting.

A Dip

Our stroll in the woods may not directly support plant restoration, but it has a significant effect on us. Imagine standing on the summit of a mountain, where a fresh breeze whispers through the gaps between the branches. When you breathe in the pure air, it feels like you are immersing yourself in Mother Nature's embrace. I would like to share a personal experience of one of my friends. They visited Shannon Falls on their return trip from Squamish after celebrating morning mass. Silence, broken only by the rushing water, filled the place, a contrast to the typical noise of people and traffic. Even now, the memory of being in the woods deeply affects him, he says. Everything felt better thanks to the crisp, refreshing air. He would proudly say that was moment of becoming one with the nature.

These meaningful experiences aid in our comprehension of the significance of trees, prompting us to engage in efforts to rejuvenate the natural world. Hikers and nature enthusiasts often grasp this concept instinctively. What deeply resonates is the connection with nature, the experience itself. At times, expressing these emotions in words can be challenging.

A dip is the feeling of getting immersed in the nature. Some people find solace in nature as a means to relax, a space to release their concerns and discover tranquility. It's like nature absorbs our troubles and gives us back a sense of calm and understanding. Experiences such as sitting under a tree, taking a stroll, hiking, or simply sitting on a balcony admiring the rustling of leaves and the chirping of birds evoke a deep appreciation for nature. These moments remind us of the vital role plants and trees play in maintaining our mental balance and overall well-being.

Waste

There must be a reason why some people can afford to live well. They might have worked for it. But we feel angry when we see waste, when we notice people throwing away things we could use. When we ponder these words, they deeply impact us regarding the wastefulness in our daily routines. I have an incident from my life that I want to share with you.

When I was in the minor seminary years ago, I had a moment that was unforgettable, bringing tears to my eyes and filling me with shame.

It was unusually calm in the refectory in the morning. The usual background noise of clinking plates and animated conversations had vanished, giving way to a profound quietness. Although the air no longer held the aroma of freshly cooked food, the tables were adorned with plates—some hardly touched, while others still had scraps of meals.

The dish is vividly etched in my memory. It was simple—neither overly seasoned nor bland. Palatable, one might say. Still, within our group of seminarians, there was a continuous habit of underestimating the importance of food. While we were free to select our meal sizes, a significant number of individuals filled their plates excessively and ended up wasting food they didn't want.

The menu didn't appeal to many people on that particular day. The majority of the boys, dissatisfied with the choices, ate what they wanted and discarded the rest into the trash. I, too, was just another of the same careless pattern.

At the time, the sight of wasted food didn't move me. I felt no shame as I contributed to the growing pile of discarded meals.

Once breakfast was finished, the priest overseeing everything asked us to come back to the dining area. On entering the refectory, the group was filled with confusion and unease noticing the waste bin positioned conspicuously next to his table.

We braced ourselves, expecting a stern reprimand or some form of punishment. The priest refrained from scolding us. He stayed without uttering a single word. His actions took us all by surprise.

He reached into the trash bin in silence, grabbed a handful of discarded food, and began consuming it.

Shocked silence enveloped the room. A number of the boys shifted their gaze uncomfortably, while others remained immobile, struggling to grasp the scene.

I experienced a profound moment of understanding. Tears welled in my eyes as I watched him. His silence communicated more effectively than words ever could. It was a poignant reminder of the dedication, love, and resources that were put into preparing the food we ended up wasting.

Ever since that day, my outlook on food has been completely different. I made a firm decision to never waste any food again. I started to serve myself only what I could consume and developed a gratitude for every meal, even if it appeared basic or boring.

Even now, years later, I feel a deep discomfort when I see food left intentionally on plates, especially in restaurants, where waste is treated so casually. It's preferable to bring home leftovers instead of throwing them away.

While this example doesn't explicitly mention the destruction of plants, the link becomes clear when considering the wider effects of food production. The production of food requires significant resources, such as water, energy, land, and labor, all of which go to waste when food is thrown away. Agriculture uses 70 percent of the world's freshwater, meaning wasting food also wastes the water used in its production and transportation. To address the rising need for food, forests are commonly cleared for farming purposes, even though a considerable amount of the food goes unconsumed. The practice indirectly leads to deforestation, ecosystem destruction, biodiversity decline, and wildlife displacement. At the same time, millions around the world are experiencing hunger and malnutrition, highlighting the glaring inequality and disregard for human needs and the earth's limited resources.

The second type of waste I want to discuss is paper and cardboard waste, which primarily originates from plants and includes a wide range of everyday products. Office paper is typically made from wood pulp or recycled plant fibers, while packaging materials, such as corrugated cardboard and paperboard boxes, are widely used for shipping and storage. Newspapers and magazines, often composed of a mix of wood pulp and recycled fibers, also contribute significantly to this waste category. Effective recycling and repurposing of these materials can help reduce their environmental impact and conserve valuable plant resources.

Clothing waste can be considered a third type of waste. The production and disposal of clothing waste made from plant-based materials, like cotton, linen, jute, and hemp, have a direct impact on plants and ecosystems. The growth of these fibers frequently results in deforestation for agricultural purposes, causing habitat destruction and loss of biodiversity. In addition, crops like cotton are highly dependent on water and the use of fertilizers and pesticides, leading to soil degradation and water pollution. Disposing of plant-based textiles in landfills causes them to decompose and produce methane, a strong greenhouse gas, whereas incineration results in carbon emissions. The excessive wastefulness hinders the sustainable use of plants and intensifies environmental deterioration, emphasizing the crucial role of mindful consumption, recycling, and sustainable fashion practices.

Human waste can increase when plant-based products are not reused or recycled. By properly handling such waste through composting, recycling, or upcycling, we can decrease environmental impact and maximize the use of plant resources.

As we conclude this section on waste, let us have words of Pope Francis for our reflection when he spoke to the general audience on the World Environmental Day. "Once our grandparents were very careful not to throw away any leftover food consumerism has led us to become accustomed to the superfluous and the daily waste of food, which we are sometimes no longer able to value correctly, as its value goes far beyond mere economic parameters Note well, though, that the food we throw away is as if we had stolen it from the table of the poor or the hungry! I invite everyone to reflect on the problem of the loss of waste of food to identity ways and methods that, addressing this issue seriously may be a vehicle for sharing and solidarity with the neediest."

Donate

The greatest threat to our planet is the belief that someone else will save it.
—Robert Swan

This way of thinking can result in doing nothing and ultimately cause damage to both the planet and ourselves. Acknowledging the need for urgency, I realize the significance of playing a vital part, either through direct involvement or by providing financial support to conservation initiatives. Providing support for these initiatives ensures the preservation of our environment.

Making donations can be a powerful way to kick-start things. Organizations can use them to research endangered plant species, carry out restoration projects, and protect crucial habitats. In addition, these funds are used for educational initiatives that promote the crucial role of plants in ecosystems and addressing climate change. Moreover, contributions help fund important projects like seed banks, tree-planting programs, and the enforcement of laws against deforestation and the illicit plant trade.

By donating, contributors give power to communities and organizations to safeguard plant biodiversity and secure a sustainable future for future generations.

Besides providing financial assistance, we can engage in conservation activities. Engaging in tree-planting events, park-restoration initiatives, and community-gardening projects coordinated by local NGOs, governments, or environmental groups can bring about tangible results. Supporting companies focused on reforestation and eco-friendly practices and advocating for green spaces in urban planning increase our impact even more. In addition, advocating for policies that support biodiversity-friendly development secures the preservation of our natural environment for the future.

Together, we can make a difference by donating, advocating, and actively participating to secure the future of our planet instead of waiting for others to take action.

Wake-Up Call

Protecting our flora is extremely urgent due to the threats posed by urbanization and rapid development, which endanger the delicate balance of nature. Realizing the necessity of preserving plant life is a wake-up call for safeguarding our ecosystems and future descendants. It concerns taking a stand against the unrestrained development pushed by powerful developers and safeguarding green spaces from being compromised for progress.

Organizing or joining workshops that concentrate on sustainable gardening and plant care is how you can begin to take action. These projects aim to educate communities about cultivating plant life, highlighting eco-friendly behaviors, and encouraging biodiversity in urban and rural settings. Besides teaching practical skills, these workshops also emphasize responsibility and the importance of plants in addressing climate change, enhancing air quality, and promoting mental health.

Communication holds just as much significance. Through the use of social media platforms and arranging community events, we can increase the reach of the message about the importance of plants in urban areas. Collective action and fostering a network of eco-conscious individuals can be achieved through sharing stories, hosting interactive discussions, and highlighting the beauty of green spaces.

The purpose of this movement is to emphasize the critical need to save our green spaces. This is a reminder to reconsider our interactions with the environment and focus on long-term sustainability instead of immediate benefits. Through the protection of our plant species and raising awareness, we create a path toward a greener and healthier planet capable of supporting life for years to come.

If we miss the wake-up call, we may not suffer the consequences immediately, but the generations to come will bear the burden. The exotic flora and fauna, once thriving, may vanish before our children have the chance to witness their beauty. Let us grasp the lifeline of sustainability before it unravels beyond repair.

Instinctual Living

Although animals, fish, and birds rely on instinct for survival, they remain within the limits of their natural behavior. For instance, you will not see a bull flying in an aircraft or a rooster sailing across the ocean. Their unique simplicity displays the beauty of their existence, underscoring our responsibility as humans. We are obligated to care for and protect animals.

Though you may know this story, let me reiterate it to enhance our understanding of the subject matter. On his wonderful farm, John Lobo cultivated various crops and raised many animals. They were largely self-sufficient, his family priding themselves on their varied and homegrown diet. The Lobos treated their animals with kindness, viewing some as family members alongside their pets. A cow, chicken, and pig were talking in the barnyard one day about their loyalty to the Lobo family.

"I have a strong preference for the Lobos, which is why I supply them with Grade A eggs for breakfast every single day. The Lobos deserve the best," the chicken declared.

"Oh yeah? You call laying some eggs commitment? That's easy stuff! *Hmm*, where do you suppose their daily supply of milk, butter, and cheese comes from?" retorted the cow.

Meanwhile, the pig listened quietly, scratching his chin with his hoof.

He finally spoke, "Let me tell you, your lives are pretty comfortable. Eggs, milk, cheese, butter—big deal. You want real commitment? My friends and I provide the bacon for breakfast and the ham for our Sunday dinner. That, ladies, is real commitment."

This story shows how animals contribute to human life in many different ways. Some animals, like the pigs, provide their total selves, serving humans through their very existence, often sacrificing their lives or essential parts of their bodies. Cows and goats, for instance, not only provide milk but also meat and leather. Honey and wax, from bees, directly and tangibly enrich human lives. Conversely, certain animals contribute to human well-being by playing essential roles in maintaining ecological balance. Earthworms enrich soil fertility, birds control pest populations, and bats pollinate plants, all of which sustain the ecosystems on which humans depend.

Direct and indirect contributions alike demonstrate the priceless connection between humans and animals. Human life depends on animals, who deserve our respect and gratitude for their complete devotion and contributions to environmental well-being.

I'm not saying we should stop eating animals, birds, or fish altogether. When we rear animals for meat, it is important to do so humanely. We must avoid causing unnecessary pain and suffering while raising them. Humane animal husbandry demonstrates both compassion for animals and respect for human values.

Animals shouldn't be killed unless it's for food. Their existence is inherently valuable; they are vital to maintaining balanced ecosystems. By treating animals with care and ensuring their survival, we contribute to a healthier, more harmonious planet for all living beings.

The foregoing paragraph covered how industries should interact with wildlife. As civilized people, we must all take responsibility to protect animals, fish, and plants. Below are some key points for reflection.

Khazan System

The Khazan system is a traditional, sustainable farming and aquaculture practice unique to Goa, India, developed centuries ago through the reclamation of coastal wetlands, salt marshes, and mangrove forests. It integrates agriculture, aquaculture, and salt farming, relying on a network of earthen levees and sluice gates to manage water flow and prevent saline intrusion. This ingenious system supports rice cultivation during the monsoon season and fish or shrimp farming in the dry season, creating a symbiotic balance between land and water use. Managed historically by local community institutions called "Gaunkaris" or "Communidades," the Khazan system exemplifies eco-friendly practices, biodiversity conservation, and efficient resource use while also mitigating flood risks and promoting soil fertility. This remarkable infrastructure, developed over three thousand years, remains vital for sustaining Goa's coastal ecosystem.

In modern times, ownership of Khazan fields is registered with individual families in the surrounding areas, and these fields continue to play a crucial role in the livelihoods of local communities. During the monsoon season, families cultivate paddy in these fields. In the summer, when aquaculture becomes viable, the fields are often auctioned for fishing rights. The highest bidder gains exclusive rights to harvest fish, while the field owners receive monetary compensation but not the fish. This dual-purpose farming system works seamlessly as, after the paddy harvest, river water is allowed to flow into the fields, creating a habitat for fish. By summer, these fields yield a bounty of fresh, tasty fish, supporting both agriculture and aquaculture.

A friend once shared an incident that underscores the importance of respecting rules and laws governing natural resources. He and his friends attempted fishing in a Khazan field during the restricted period without permission from the auction winner. When confronted, the auction holder said, "If I came to your property and stole, how would you feel?" This remark resonated deeply, making them realize the significance of fairness and the need to respect legal ownership. Similarly, abiding by laws related to animals, fish, and birds is vital for their protection and the preservation of biodiversity. These laws prevent cruelty, overexploitation, and habitat destruction while promoting sustainable coexistence. Illegal activities like unregulated fishing, poaching, and habitat destruction disrupt ecosystems and threaten species survival. By respecting these laws and established practices, we contribute to maintaining ecological balance, safeguarding the rights of those who depend on these systems and ensuring the long-term sustainability of both the Khazan system and the broader natural world.

Recycle

Protecting fauna is significantly aided by recycling role in pollution reduction and habitat conservation. Recycling materials, such as plastic, metal, and paper, reduces the need to extract raw materials, thus protecting wildlife habitats and ecosystems from damage caused by deforestation, mining, and oil drilling. Decreased landfill and ocean waste from recycling prevents animals from ingesting or becoming entangled in harmful debris, thus avoiding injury or death. Recycling mitigates climate change, a serious threat to biodiversity, by lowering the energy and emissions used to create new materials. Recycling helps create a cleaner, healthier environment, which protects the ecosystems animals depend on to survive.

Good intentions, no matter how noble, remain futile unless they are put into action. A grandmother I knew had a terrible habit of hoarding things. Her intention behind this habit was never malicious; rather, she believed she was safeguarding valuable items for future use—a future she envisioned where these things would serve a purpose or come to someone's aid. She felt safer with each new possession, picturing a future where it helped her or a family member.

Her habit of accumulating possessions, however, only worsened over time. She would store away clothes, utensils, old furniture, newspapers, and other random objects, always thinking, This *might be useful someday*. Over time, her house became a cluttered mess of unused items and forgotten treasures. While intending to conserve resources, she failed to put them to any practical use.

The grandmother's possessions, gathered over a lifetime, were tragically considered worthless by others after her passing. The family, emotionally detached from her possessions, decided to burn or dispose of most of them without a second thought. What she treasured and lovingly safeguarded was nothing but ashes, devoid of purpose.

This story serves as a touching reminder of the insufficiency of good intentions. Even the best intentions are useless without practical applications. The grandmother's well-intentioned hoarding ultimately proved unproductive. It emphasizes the importance of acting on one's intentions rather than letting them accumulate like stagnant clutter. Good intentions must always be coupled with meaningful actions; otherwise, they remain as futile as the hoard of unused items—destined to perish without value or impact.

Recycling requires immediate action; avoid delaying or stockpiling. Rather than accumulating items for a potential future use, we should prioritize repurposing, recycling, or donating items. Hoarding doesn't just make our spaces messy; it also reduces the worth of things that could help others or be used for something useful. We need to act now to recycle; otherwise, we'll waste resources and create a disorganized, meaningless environment.

Conclusion

I would like to begin this conclusion with a profound quote by St. Teresa of Avila: "It helped me to look at fields, or water, or flowers. In these things, I found a remembrance of the Creator." This quote serves as a beautiful reminder of the divine presence manifested in nature. God is both the Alpha and the Omega, the Beginning and the End. By His divine will, all things are created and their continued existence is solely dependent on His desire. From mountains to flowers and all creatures great and small, creation reveals the Creator's magnificent power.

Humanity has been given the responsibility of caring for creation. We are the stewards of the earth, responsible for safeguarding the flora and fauna that God has so graciously provided. Nurturing and protecting nature isn't just a responsibility; it's a sacred duty. Divine craftsmanship is shown in creation's beauty, a beauty we, as caretakers, must preserve for future generations.

Exploiting nature's resources without sustainable practices, or ignoring nature altogether, violates this divine trust. When we protect nature, we honor the Creator. Our actions toward environmental sustainability—planting trees, preserving life—reflect our role as caretakers of creation.

Therefore, we must remember our responsibility to safeguard and cherish nature. By observing nature's wonders, we can glimpse the Creator, inspiring a commitment of preserving its beauty and balance. We thus meet our moral and spiritual responsibilities and maintain earth as a vibrant, life-sustaining home for all.

We encounter God's greatness in nature and express our gratitude through compassionate stewardship of creation. In harmony with nature, let us cherish this divine gift and preserve it as an inheritance for future generations. I would conclude this chapter with a positive paragraph from the *Encyclical Letter Laudato Si'* of the Holy Father Francis on the care for our common home "Yet all is not lost. Human beings, while capable of the worst, are also capable of rising above themselves, choosing again what is good, and making a new start, despite their mental and social conditioning. We are able to take an honest look at ourselves, to acknowledge our deep dissatisfaction, and to embark on new paths to authentic freedom. No system can completely suppress our openness to what is good, true and beautiful, or our God-given ability to respond to his grace at work deep in our hearts. I appeal to everyone throughout the world not to forget this dignity which is ours. No one has the right to take it from us."

CREATOR AND STEWARD

In the beginning, the God spoke,
And life from nothing gently woke.
The sun was illumined, the stream ran,
The earth was rocking in His plan.
Mountains raised tall, valleys lay low,
Woodland would flourish, and rivers would flow.

The sky was brushed with shades so bright,
Stars ornamented the velvet night.
Birds obtained wings, the seas swayed,
Beasts of the meadows and marine life He made.
Flowers blossomed in radiant array,
In thanksgiving to the creator, day after day.

Then He formed with love, the crown of His land,
Humankind, after His own image and with His hand.
"Care for my creatures," the Creator said,
"Protect it with love, where life has tread."
The responsibility was given, distinct and true,
To guard the earth and all life too.

But the heart of man cold and blind,
Greed and arrogance contaminated the mind.
Forests knock down, and rivers wept,
Beasts slaughtered, the oceans slept.
Toxic gas conquered the air, the waters turned gray,
Creation lamented as hope slipped away.

Yet in the brokenness, a sigh arose,
A wispier of conscience that softly grows.
"We are the stewards, not owners of land,
We must heal it with heart and hand."
So men and women with acumen and care,
Began to retain and restore the world in despair.

General Conclusion

As Pope Francis reminds us in his encyclical letter *Laudato Si'*: "We have forgotten that we ourselves are dust of the earth (cf. Gen. 2:7); our very bodies are made up of her elements, we breathe her air and we receive life and refreshment from her waters."

Rich or poor, one day death will inevitably knock at the door of our body and knock us down, taking our breath away. Life and death are two sides of the same coin—whatever comes to life must eventually fade away. If we are uncertain about the duration of our own existence, how can we presume control over the lives of other creatures? We must allow other living beings to coexist along with us. This does not mean putting hold on development or abstaining from meat consumption but rather recognizing that God has provided these living beings for our needs, not for our greed and to use and not abuse.

Since the dawn of human civilization, humankind has been inextricably linked with nature. Our most primitive ancestors depended on the natural world for survival. To meet their basic needs, they hunted animals for food, walked miles in search of plants suitable for eating, and used natural resources to design tools and erect shelter. Early humans did not see themselves as detached from nature; they understood their place within it and esteemed its rhythms. Their connection to nature was deeply embedded in their traditions, art, and way of life.

However, with the increase of industry and technology, this intrinsic acquaintance has weakened. Humanity has developed a sense of supremacy over nature, perceiving it as a resource to be subjugated rather than a home to be cherished. This shift has led to relentless environmental crises, including deforestation, toxic waste, and climate change.

Yet, in spite of these challenges, hope remains. In recent years, consciousness of environmental conservation has grown, stirring efforts to restore our relationship with nature. From grassroots activities to global initiatives, individuals and organizations worldwide are striving to protect our planet and generate a sustainable future. By recognizing our role as stewards rather than conquerors, we can rebuild a harmonious coexistence with the natural world—one rooted in respect, balance, and care for our common home.

I wish to end this work with a quote from St. Augustine of Hippo: "Some people, in order to discover God, read books. But there is a great book: the very appearance of created things. Look above you! Look below you! Read it. God, whom you want to discover, never wrote that book with ink. Instead, He set before your eyes the things that He had made. Can you ask for a louder voice than that?"

I wish to end this general conclusion with few lines of prayer in union with creation from the *Encyclical Letter Laudato Si'* of the Holy Father Francis on the care for our common home.

> Father, we praise you with all your creatures.
> They came forth from your all-powerful hand ...
> Today you are alive in every creature in your risen glory ...
> Triune Lord, wondrous community of infinite love, teach us to contemplate you
> in the beauty of the universe, for all things speak of you ...
> Enlighten those who possess power and money that they may avoid the sin of indifference,
> that they may love the common good, advance the weak, and care for this world in which we live ...

The prayer begins by praising God the Father for creating all things, recognizing that all creatures come from His hand and are filled with His love. It moves to praise Jesus Christ, the Son, who became part of the earth through the incarnation and now lives in all creation in His risen glory. Then it honors the Holy Spirit, who guides creation toward God and dwells within human hearts, inspiring good works.

The prayer then addresses the Triune God as a community of infinite love, asking for the grace to see God in the beauty of the universe. It calls for a deeper connection with all creatures and a sense of responsibility toward them.

Finally, the prayer becomes a plea: that those in power may be moved by love and not indifference, that justice and care for the earth may prevail, and that God's Kingdom of peace and beauty may come. It ends in a spirit of praise and hope.

www.ingramcontent.com/pod-product-compliance
Lightning Source LLC
Jackson TN
JSHW081014260825
90001JS00003B/4